# Introduction to Designing

# Introduction to Designing

Shailendra Sengar

ANMOL PUBLICATIONS PVT. LTD.
NEW DELHI-110 002 (INDIA)

**ANMOL PUBLICATIONS PVT. LTD.**
*H.O.:* 4374/4B, Ansari Road, Darya Ganj,
New Delhi-110 002 (India)
Ph.: 23278000, 23261597

*B.O.:* No. 1015, Ist Main Road, BSK IIIrd Stage
IIIrd Phase, IIIrd Block
Bangalore - 560 085 (India)
Visit us at: www.anmolpublications.com

*Introduction to Designing*



First Published, 2008

ISBN 978-81-261-3435-9

PRINTED IN INDIA

---

Printed at Mehra Offset Press, Delhi.

# Contents

# Preface

This Encyclopaedic Series of Career and Vocational Guidance Covers careers, describing jobs, places of employment, working conditions, qualifications, education and training. This has been developed to aid career and counsellors and job placement coordinators in planning activities for students and potential students about career vocational education programs. It contains a career and vocational guidance model which clarifies what career and vocational guidance services mean and what planners should include in their activities. The model shows an interrelatedness among major thrusts with career development being a central theme of vocational guidance. All of the thrusts depicted in the model represent essential services that should be available to students in career and vocational education programs. The encyclopaedia deals with various sections which correspond to the major thrusts identified in the model: (1) career development; (2) recruitment; (3) guidance and counselling; (4) placement; (5) follow-up and follow-through; and (6) consultation. Each section contains an outline of the perceived needs of the topic, an overview of the topic relative to career and vocational guidance, and some suggested activities and strategies that may be useful in meeting student needs.

It also contains current information about occupations, employment trends, and job searching. Materials on career decision-making, internships, and salaries are also located in each volume. This Series of Encyclopaedia helps students assess their potential for various careers.

*Shailendra Sengar*

1

# Career in Fashion Designing

## The Fashion Industry

The fashion industry is huge. Each year, over $250 billion is spent on fashion (including accessories) in the United States and over $20 billion in revenue is generated annually. Over 4 million people are employed in this industry which includes the following areas: design, manufacturing, distribution, marketing, retailing, advertising, communications, publishing and consulting.

Fashion industry employers are located just about everywhere but most are concentrated in New York City (with over 5,000 showrooms), California (Los Angeles and San Francisco), Miami, London, Paris and Italy. Large employers are based in cities such as Dallas (Neiman Marcus, Fossil), Ohio (Limited Brands) and Beaverton, or (Nike). While some production still occurs in the United States and Europe, the majority is now done overseas (China, India, Mexico, South America). To compete in the fashion industry job market today, job seekers must have strong computer/technical skills (Excel, Photoshop, Illustrator, Quark Xpress) and understand the global economy, including manufacturing and textile technology.

*Sample Job Titles*

*Bachelor's Degree / Entry Level*

*Further Education / Experience Often Required*

*product coordinator*

*media sales executive*

*marketing representative*
*advertising copywriter*
*assistant buyer*
*operations manager*
*fashion coordinator*
*public relations executive*
*market research trainee*
*market researcher*
*merchandise manager*
*textile merchandising executive*
*imaging assistant*
*fashion editor*

## Fashion Designing

Fashion designers develop new styles and products for clothing apparel and accessories by creating original designs or by adapting fashions to suit local conditions, trends and buyers. They are the ones who approve final samples before they go into production. The designer begins the designing process only after thorough market research, *i.e.*, understanding the needs of the client/market in terms of changing trends, budget etc. Accessory Designers specialise in designing shoes, bags, scarves, jewellery, ties, etc. which complete the look of the garment.

Personal Attributes: Fashion designers need to be artistic, creative and must posses ability to translate ideas in sketches, must have keen sense of colour *i.e.* combination of shades and tones, visual imagination & knowledge of market trends.

Educational Qualification: Basic qualification for a course in fashion designing is 10+2, it varies depending on the course chosen.

Job Prospectus: They can find employment with professional designers as apprentices, with manufacturing units, export houses, boutiques, media as costume designers, freelancing for fashion houses and boutiques and at the same time it is a rewarding possibility for self employment by opening your own boutique.

Fashion coordinators arrange and supervise the marketing of fashion clothing for manufacturing houses, textile firms and retail stores. It is a highly competitive job involving a variety of functions. They advice on latest fashion trends, organise fashion shows, assist in advertising *i.e.* promoting sales and liaison with fabric dealers to ensure that the fabric, buttons and colours are of the correct shade, quality and design. Coordinates may be required to travel widely to get an idea of the fashion trends.

Personal Attributes: Must have high level of artistic and creative talents, a natural flair for fashion, sound judgement, excellent communication and organisational skills.

Illustrator draw free hand sketches of designers ideas. They not only need outstanding sketching skills but at the same time requires excellent communication skills. Illustrator at times has to discuss with customers when new collection is introduced and this requires ability to interact.

He/she is a much sought-after person by big garment houses and organisations.

Fashion Consultant must be aware of the trends and transitions in the fashion market along with knowledge about fashion designing. They are expected to offer ideas regularly on how to further develop a product to be readily absorbed in a market. He/she should be a sharp observer sensitive to changing trends.

Cutting Assistants have to cut samples according to specifications of the designer. A cutting assistant cuts samples, makes and alters patterns to see that the design visualised can be converted to a real dress.

Sketching Assistants make the technical sketches of the garments and makes drawings for presentation. It is from this specification sketches one decide how a garment has to be fabricated. The sketching assistant sometimes have to the select the fabric also.

Fashion Stylist has to coordinate the entire wardrobe for a fashion show or programme to promote the sales of the products. It involves coordinating the dress, accessories, make up, hairstyle, even the colour of the nail polish of the model according to the theme and the overall look of the show. Sometimes a stylist is even involved in fabric selection. He/ she has to be well versed in the trends and happenings in the industry and also have a keen sense of current fashion trends.

### *Textile Designing*

***Textile Designer or Fabric Designer:*** Designs woven, knitted or printed fabrics for clothing and other home ware items like carpets, tableware etc. They treat the yarn through different types of processes to give it a particular finish. The textile designer also make drawings of initial concepts and work with various yarns and fabrics taking into account the final use of the fabric by translating the designs into marketable fabrics.

Textile designers work within and alongside industries such as fashion, interior design and textiles. They may also work under professional designers or as freelance designers working with a client base.

Colourist play a vital role in the textile-printers, artist team. They are involved in block printing or machine printing. They must keep a record of colour samples and fabric pieces and have to work in a high paced environment, to meet deadlines. The colourist has to be very organised and must carefully follow precise instructions.

The other career options in textile designing are weavers, embroidery designers, dying & printing consultant, fabric analyser, textile lab manager, fabric resource manager etc.

### *Apparel Merchandising*

Fashion Merchandisers are mainly responsible for marketing. He/she has to study past and current sales data and analyse trends. They have to collect specifications from the buyers, coordinate with fashion designers and production team to develop a product which meets market requirement. They must have knowledge of fashion trends, textures, materials and colours on one hand and understanding of market demand and the production processes on the other. At the same time have analytical ability and communication skills.

They can find employment with garment industries, export houses, manufacturing firms etc.

Visual merchandising a comparatively new career field which has sprung up with the growing popularity of window and floor displays. Visual merchandisers main area of work is to create impressive window displays. They can find employment with fashion boutiques, shopping malls, emporia etc. They are also engaged as shop floor managers. They can also do freelancing on contract basis for window displays in exhibitions, fairs and other places.

Other career options under this head are production coordinator, quality control supervisor, fashion retailer, export manager etc.

### *Fashion Journalism and Presentation*

**Fashion Journalist** is an overall in-charge of a fashion magazine. It is through them that the general public gets to know the latest fashion trends.

He/she should have excellent taste for fashion and keep themselves abreast with latest fashion news, consumer reaction to new collections, fashion shows, current and future trends in colour, design and fabric. Today fashion journalist has a bright scope for employment as there is a need for exclusive articles and programmes with the development of fashion industry.

Fashion Photography is an extremely creative and well paid profession. Fashion photographer needs to have a keen eye for aesthetic detail, a thorough knowledge of cameras and the technicalities involved in taking pictures, of light, distance and perspective to be successful. He/she should be inventive and able to visualise and communicate his ideas, at the same time must be sensitive to the moods of the models and interact freely with them. Fashion photography is one of the choices that photographers can diversify into. They can do freelancing and find employment with fashion houses, designers, fashion journals and news papers.

Modelling If you have an attractive and outgoing personality and good communication skills, you can opt for modelling. Modelling is a highly paid job and is categorised into live modelling and photographic modelling. Live modelling is what we see in fashion shows, exhibitions where models display clothes and accessories for potential customers. Photographic or still modelling is taking photographs for Magazines, newspapers, catalogues and films for advertisements. One must take care to maintain their figure and looks, as modelling is a highly competitive field. Good looks, height, an attractive physique combined with self confidence and a trendy approach to life goes a long way to make a model popular. In addition they should be highly photogenic. Patience and the ability to stand criticism are vital for survival and progress.

Models can find employment with designers, in design houses, advertisement firms etc.

Fashion Stylist has to coordinate the entire wardrobe for a fashion show or programme to promote the sales of the products. It involves coordinating the dress, accessories, make up, hairstyle, even the colour of the nail polish of the model according to the theme and the overall look of the show. Sometimes a stylist is even involved in fabric selection. He/she has to be well versed in the trends and happenings in the industry and also have a keen sense of current fashion trends.

### *Design a Career in Fashion*

Ready, set, style! If you're one of those people who haunts the retail clothing stores, has a closet bursting with the latest styles and who can't resist offering wardrobe advice, a career in fashion design may be right up your alley. If you've got creativity, perseverance and an artistic flair to boot, you're on your way.

However, if you're hoping to achieve status as a "fashion diva," then you'll need to work hard to establish a reputation and a clientele for your designs, as the market for designer fashion is competitive and fast-paced—but achievable if you've got what it takes! For those who reach the apex of this industry, the rewards can be phenomenal.

***What it Takes?:*** The fashion industry is all about creativity, skill, awareness of trends and a good business sense. Hoping to work normal hours? Plan on designing clothing lines for the masses in the apparel manufacturing business — think retail, baby! If you manage to build a good name for yourself, you could cater to high-end department stores and specialty boutiques.

Want to give Armani a run for his money? Anticipate being your own boss and catering solely to individual clients. Fame brings some drawbacks, though. You'll likely work unusual hours to meet the needs of your clients. Whatever the venue, though, you'll be one of the people who decides if black is *really* the new black.

***Rising to the Top:*** To be competitive, you'll need more than great style to land a job in fashion design. Basic artistic skills are required, as are a refined aesthetic sense and at a minimum, a two- or four-year degree in fashion design, art, or other related field. Several universities offer degrees in the arts, but there are various fashion and design schools offering associate's, bachelor's and master's degrees in areas related specifically to fashion design and the creative arts industries.

Many of these schools enjoy first-rate reputations and are an excellent way for you to earn an industry-specific degree with course selections and specialized studies that include everything from garment construction to fashion merchandising. The industry is highly competitive since it draws on a tremendous amount of talented individuals just like you seeking employment in the market. Demonstrated skill is the thing that will set you above other candidates when hiring decisions are made. (That and a great wardrobe!)

***Are you in?:*** All those years of fashion advice to your friends and "designer" clothes pieced together on your mother's old Singer machine could pay off with panache and determination. You might not land the Miami Beach mansion, but you won't be hurting to pay your bills, either. In 2004, mid-range salaries were in the low sixties, depending on location and the company. The top 10 percent of designers in the biz bring home over $100,000 a year. Exclusive designers—well...how do you feel about mooring your own yacht...right next to your Miami Beach mansion?

### *Fashion Design*

The word 'fashion' immediately conjures up images of glitz and glamour. And many young people, attracted by these attributes decide to foray into fashion only to realise that what they see outside is not the inside story. Admittedly, there are some glamorous aspects to this business. As part of the fash frat (fashion fraternity for the uninformed), you may get to rub shoulders with the rich and famous, but reaching there is sheer hard work.

***The Work:*** Fashion Design can be divided into three main branches—Garment design, Leather design, Accessory & Jewellery design. Here we will focus on Garment design.

While the saying "clothes make the a man" merits debate, the fact is we no longer wear clothes to keep ourselves covered or warm, but to express our personality and "attitude". This is where the fashion designer steps in, to help us make the correct fashion statement. Creating a style, using the right fabric, the right cut and a good finish, the designer turns out either a singular creation (one of its kind) that may sell for a king's ransom, or more usually, outfits that will reach a retail outlet in different sizes and colours. In certain cases, the garment may even be mass-produced for a specific market.

Garments include items of regular clothing, generally western style, although there is a growing local market for Indian style designer wear such as salwar-kameez, sherwanis, ghagra-cholis, kurtis and so on. There are four courses of action that you can adopt to launch into the career of your dreams:

Lawyers in private practice usually work for long and irregular hours meeting clients, researching and reading about new:

- Apprenticeship under a flourishing, well-known designer.
- Employment in an export house or garment manufacturing unit.
- Freelancing for fashion houses and boutiques.
- Self-employment, as in opening your boutique or manufacturing unit or an export outfit to showcase your talent.

Nothing can compare with the absolute joy when your creation is admired and appreciated for its style and finish. And the high-voltage publicity and applause as you proceed for the curtain call at the end of a stunning show won't hurt either. Today fashion designers share equal space on Page 3 as models and film stars.

***What it Takes?:*** A question often asked by young people is whether they really need to be trained to be a designer. Most young people who are able to sketch well and have an interest in fashion believe their talent and interest already qualifies them for the fashion industry. But fashion design is not just about sketching pretty clothes. Barring a few exceptions where talent borders on genius, it is certainly recommended that you pursue a course in fashion design. And you can do so straight after school. There are a variety of courses available to suit different needs and budgets.

While the academic requirements are not very high, you need considerable aptitude and talent to be labelled "designer" material. You must be highly creative to combine colours, shades and textures and express your ideas through sketches.

If you can visualise designs and enjoy working with fabrics and accessories you are looking at the right career. Along with fashion consciousness and creativity, you also need excellent communication skills to articulate your ideas and understand the client's requirements. Knowledge of the market and a good eye for detail are the other must-haves.

Beware, though fashion is as much about technique as about style. You need to be clued in on manufacturing technology, time and motion studies, plant efficiency, labour motivation, zero-defect production—all are extremely relevant to this industry.

Before you become a name to reckon with, be prepared to put in tons of hard work and running around.

However, fashion design is just one of the many careers that a student of fashion design prepares for. There are a number of others such as marketing and merchandising, fashion coordination, fashion journalism, etc.

***Employment Opportunities:*** In India, the fashion industry has just begun to come of age. As it is still in its fledgling stage, it offers plenty of opportunities for enthusiastic, talented and hard working youngsters.

Prospects for fashion design graduates are pretty good thanks to the huge and still growing demand for "designer wear" and the equally large volume of exports. What with the sheer variety and availability of materials–from traditional silks and ikats to jamawars and handlooms in vibrant weaves and dyes – India is a fashion designer's dream.

Until a few years ago, there was not a single Indian name in the global fashion scene. However with the establishment of NIFT and some other fashion schools, a band of gifted designers is already making its mark on the fashion firmament. Today names like Ritu Kumar, Ritu Beri, Rohit Bal, Sunit Verma, J.J. Vallaya and Tarun Tahiliani have virtually become household names–what with the media show-casing their talent across double-page spreads in glossy mags and sundry fashion-related programmes on TV.

***What you'll Make?:*** The fancy salaries and the hype that you read about in the glossies is only for those who are really talented to begin with or those passing out of the premier institutes. For the rest, finding a decent toehold can be pretty tough. Also considering the fact that just about everyone is rushing into fashion designing, it may be wise to opt for some of the other courses like Merchandising, Accessory Designing, Garment Manufacturing Technology, etc., all of which have a component of fashion design in them.

Having said that, the money is pretty good. As a fresher you'll start out with a monthly package of Rs.8,000-14,000. A couple of years down as your designing skills mature, your salary would be in the range of Rs.30,000-40,000. Of course, if you become a marquee designer and are lucky enough to go international, you could for a single creation, quite literally ask for the moon!

***Where to Study?:*** Your race for admission into a reputed fashion school will begin straight after school. Subjects like drawing, painting, home science, computer graphics will develop your creativity.

By the time you finish the course you will have mastered the step-by-step production of a garment — from designing to pattern making, production and even marketing.

Although, if you are interested in further specialisation to work in a large manufacturing unit or start your own fabrication unit someday, you could opt for postgraduate courses in garment manufacture, merchandising, etc.

When we talk of fashion, we often forget the wide range of accessories that also constitute fashion. Although the courses listed here mainly pertain to apparel design, you could opt for a course in accessory design or specifically in jewellery design, knitwear design, footwear design or leather design — the options are as diverse as the range and variety of accessories themselves.

Fashion design programmes prepare people to design clothing for commercial sale. Students learn to create designs both manually and using computers. They also learn about management in the fashion industry.

Are you obsessed with fashion? Do you flip through fashion magazines and watch fashion shows, all the while envisioning your own designs on the models? Do you feel you have a unique sense of style? Do you prefer to design your own clothes rather than buy the standard fare in clothing stores? Do you fantasize about creating costumes for theatre and film?

If you answered "yes" to any of those questions, then fashion design may be the programme of study for you. As a fashion designer, you use your artistic abilities to design all kinds of apparel and accessories, from underwear to outer-wear, hats to shoes.

You could work on producing your designs as well. You might supervise a team of people or even take up some scissors and do your own cutting and sewing. You could also design clothing under a particular brand name or develop your own brand.

As a student in this programme, you learn to combine your artistic sensibility with technical skills. You study the properties of different types of fabrics and fibers. You learn fashion design techniques, using both computer technology and traditional methods. You also learn about the history of fashion and study the ways that culture has influenced fashion trends.

Nearly 140 schools offer programmes in fashion or apparel design. You can earn a certificate or an associate's degree. You can also earn a bachelor's degree. After high school, a certificate usually takes one year of full-time study and an associate's degree typically takes two. A bachelor's degree usually takes four years."

***College Preparation:*** Proprietary schools, colleges and universities all offer this programme. If you want to study at a proprietary school, you can prepare for this programme of study by completing your high school degree or getting a GED. If you want to study at a college or university, you can prepare for this programme by taking the following courses: four years of English, three years of math, three years of social studies and two years of science. Some colleges also require two years of a second language.

*Introduction to Business*

*General Computer Applications*

*Computer Graphics*

*Clothing and Sewing*

*CAD Design and Software*

*Art*

*Drawing and Painting*

*Art Portfolio*

*Marketing*

*Clothing and Textiles*

***Undergraduate Special***

You should also complete college-level courses in the following:

- Art Appreciation
- Design (beginning and advanced levels)
- Drawing (beginning and advanced levels)

Most schools require the submission of a portfolio that shows your drawing skills and capacity for creating both artistic and functional apparel. Portfolio requirements vary."

### *Typical Course Work*

This undergraduate programme typically includes courses in the following subjects:

- Apparel Construction
- Apparel Design and Development
- Business Law
- Colour Theory
- Computer-Aided Design (CAD) for Apparel
- Draping
- Fashion Presentation
- History of Fashion
- International Marketing
- Line Development
- Pattern Development
- Portfolio Development
- Principles of Fit
- Principles of Marketing
- Principles of Visual Communication
- Social-Psychological Aspects of Clothing
- Tailoring Techniques
- Textiles: Fibres and Yarns
- Textiles: Structures, Dyes and Finishes

### *Things to Know*

Many fashion designers are self-employed. For this reason, you may find it helpful to take courses in business, marketing and accounting.

Earning an associate degree in fashion design may only qualify you to be a designer's assistant. A bachelor's degree, including general education and liberal arts course work, suggests that you have more qualifications and are more competent in design.

Some programmes offer study-abroad opportunities, giving you the chance to study fashion in cities that are often considered to be fashion capitals. These cities might include Paris, London and Milan.

### *Fashion/Apparel Design*

If you've ever dreamed of a career in fashion, a graduate or professional programme in fashion design will help bring your head down out of the clouds and land you on the runway. A fashion-design student studies elements like colour, fabric choice and silhouette (are skinny pants right for this season?). Additionally, you'll gain technical proficiency in computer-aided design and garment construction, pattern-making, draping and sewing. You should carefully consider your career goals when evaluating M.F.A. programmes, which will either take a creative or technical approach–do you want to be a designer or production manager? Or do fashion merchandising or fashion illustration appeal to you? Make sure that the school's curriculum will meet your future plans.

Classes are extremely hands-on and have students sketching, sewing and drafting from day one. You can expect to create original garments and present them in a public exhibition or a runway show. Most institutions encourage students to supplement their education with an internship, which is helpful — maybe even essential—in making connections and landing a first job. School location, facilities and alumni connections should also be factors to consider when researching programmes.

***Degree Information:*** M.F.A. and M.A. programmes in fashion design are extremely rare; four-year bachelor's programmes are much more common. There are also many certificate and associate's programmes that provide students (with or without a bachelor's degree) with enough basic technical and/or design training to make a career change. These one- or two-year programmes are excellent options for someone without prior fashion experience who wants to break into the industry. Students can opt for a vocational school, which focus more on technical skills and prepare students for careers in the mass market (think everyday clothing at the mall), or an art school, which offers more creative classes and prepares students for careers in the higher-end market (think Paris and the runway). Most graduate, undergraduate and technical programmes require a senior thesis or project, which generally means the creation and presentation of a collection in a runway show; some also require a professional internship.

Questions to Ask Yourself When Choosing a Degree Programme:

- Are you interested in designing outrageous, creative garments or things more appropriate for everyday wear? Does the programme emphasize creativity and experimentation or technical and business skills?
- Does the school have industry connections? A good reputation within the national and international fashion industry?
- Do students present their work in a publicly-attended runway show? What percentage of students get to participate?
- What are the experience and connections of the faculty? How does their work fit into your areas of interest?
- Are you willing to relocate to a major city for school and/ or a job? (New York City equals better fashion connections than Salt Lake City, for example.)

## Career Plans in Fashion

A career in fashion could take you in any of a number of exciting directions. One thing fashion careers share, aside from being a rewarding outlet for your creative talents, is their beginning: fashion school.

Study fashion and you'll be rewarded with a wealth of practical information that will give you the knowledge, the credentials and the all-important portfolio that you'll need to get that crucial entry-level position in the fashion industry.

### *Choosing the Right Course*

The fashion industry is competitive, particularly so in fashion design and success depends as much upon hard work and dedication as on natural talent. To make the most of your commitment and enthusiasm for fashion, it's important to choose the right course.

General fashion courses provide a grounding in the principles of fashion; thereafter, you can pursue specialized study or training. Some fashion schools offer a broad programme and expect you to specialize on your own once you enter the field. Others are entirely focused on a certain part of the industry – fashion design or fashion merchandising, for example. You can get a real head start by specializing from the outset if you already know which part of the fashion industry you want to work in.

### *Careers in Fashion*

Fashion careers are essentially of two types – those in fashion design and those in the sales and marketing side of the industry. The skills necessary for fashion design and fashion merchandising are quite different, although to master one requires a good understanding of the other.

Both sides of the fashion industry are competitive and require creative talent and usually at least a bachelor's degree, so you should expect to work hard to get ahead. The rewards are excellent. Not only is the work varied and interesting with plenty of opportunity for self-employment, you can expect good financial rewards too.

*What does it mean to study Fashion?*

If you decide to study for a fashion career, you'll learn to design clothing and accessories or the fabrics and materials they're made of.

*What kind of person does well in Fashion careers?*

### *Career in Fashion Designer*

***A Day in the Life:*** Ever wonder what Giorgio Armani, Betsey Johnson, Donna Karan and Ralph Lauren do all the time? Work! Few other professions depend so much on keeping on top of fickle popular opinion and watching what competitors produce. The life of a designer is intimately linked to tastes and sensibilities that change at a moment's notice and he or she must be able to capitalize on or—even better—influence those opinions. Designers reflect society's sensibilities through clothing design. "You have to know just about everything that's been done before so that you can recognize it when it becomes popular again," wrote one respondent.

Fashion designers are involved in every phase of designing, showing and producing all types of clothing, from bathing suits to evening gowns. Those with talent, vision, determination and ambition can succeed in this difficult, demanding and highly competitive industry. Fashion design can be more glamorous than a 1940s Hollywood musical or drearier than a bank statement, but it's always taxing. A designer's day includes reading current fashion magazines, newspapers and other media that reflect current trends and tastes. He or she looks at materials, attends fashion shows and works with other designers on projects.

A designer should be able to communicate his or her philosophy, vision and capabilities clearly and comprehensively through sketches, discussions and, occasionally, samples. No matter what his or her personal style is, a designer must produce a creative, exciting and profitable product line. As in most professions that produce superstars, it is easy for a competent but otherwise unremarkable designer to wallow in obscurity, designing small pieces of collections, generic lines (the plain white boxer short, for example), or specialties (cuffs, ruffles, etc.). The personality that raises itself above this level must be as large as the vision of the designer; perhaps that's why the word "crazy" showed up in more than 75 percent of our surveys as a plus in fashion design.

***Paying Your Dues:*** People entering the field should have a good eye for colour, style and shape, an ability to sketch and some formal preparation in design. An excellent portfolio is a must for the job search. A two- or four-year degree in fashion design is helpful, as is knowledge of textiles and a familiarity with the quirks of a variety of fabrics, but no formal certification is required. Candidates should have a working knowledge of business and marketing. The hours are long for a fashion designer and the initial pay is very limited. This is one of those hit-or-miss occupations where beginners work as someone's assistant until, when they can muster up enough confidence in their abilities and sell that confidence to their superiors, they design a few pieces themselves. The superstar rise is an unlikely event, but it happens. Based on the number of "international star designers" in the last 10 years and the number of people who have entered the profession, the estimated odds of becoming an internationally famous designer are roughly 160,000:1.

***Associated Careers:*** Fashion designers who become unhappy with the lifestyle (low pay, long hours, hard work, low chance of advancement) leave the field to do a variety of things. Some of them use their colour and design skills to become interior designers, graphic designers, or fashion consultants. More than one quarter of the people who leave remain in the clothing industry, either on the production end or on the institutional buying end. Another 10 percent of them enter the advertising or promotions industry.

### *Is Fashion Design for You?*

***I want to be a Fashion Designer:*** How do I get started? What should I know and how will I find out? Should I go to school or try to get a job? Do I want to start my own company? So many questions in my head, where do I start and where will I end up? Sound like you? I remember the feeling exactly like that myself!

I've learned a lot about the industry since I began and I'm still finding out there is always more to know. I've worked for giant manufacturers and I've made one of a kind pieces for private clientele. I've had my own label and my own store. I've sold other peoples clothes. I've been unemployed and I've had great jobs that I've left for even better ones. I've realized that it's an industry where art is joined and, in fact, led by commerce. Some people have made it in a very short time with no training and others have graduated from university with degrees before climbing their career ladders. I started in fine arts, then fashion design and am now the chairperson and teacher at a fashion design programme.

Where are your answers? After witnessing both success and failure, I believe that most importantly you must first discover if this is really what you want to do! Start by getting involved in this industry. Your local mall probably has someone on staff that's involved in fashion show production and fashion promotion. Make an appointment and let them know what you're interested in and volunteer to help on the next project. This is a great introduction to the glitz and glamour side of the business, however, you will still need to get a broader picture.

Look for a store in your neighbourhood that makes and sells its own clothes and see if you can meet the owner and a designer (often one in the same). Try to talk your way into a tour of their studio or factory or ask for the opportunity to see what a typical day is like. Ask as many questions as you can from as many people as possible: this will help you gain a real sense of the industry.

Ask about the hours they work, how long it took them to get their own store, if they went to school, what were their greatest hurdles, what is the toughest part of the job, you get the picture. Some may be too busy preparing for a show or new clothing line, but don't be discouraged. You really should make every effort to get a feel for the business-I assure you it's not all catwalks and photoshoots.

If you still want to be a fashion designer, then dig in some more. Go to your local fabric store and see if they offer any lessons, or try buying some fabric and making something for yourself. Contact your local community college to see what courses or programmes they offer in fashion. Check to see if they have any visiting professionals that are willing to give a workshop or talk at your school. I know the International Academy of Design in Toronto offers an intensive two-week summer studio, perhaps your local school has something similiar. Check out books on fashion design at your local library. Don't forget the Internet: it is a wealth of fashion information waiting to be tapped into.

Alana Berry and Alexander Labayen, both former students of Toronto's International Academy of Design, have taken somewhat different approaches to world of fashion design.

Before studying fashion, Alana pursued a career in business and feels it is the best thing she could have done. "When I look at the big picture now, I realize it's not just about being creative: fashion is also a business. If I didn't have a strong understanding of business, it would all be just a hobby."

Once she realized that fashion was calling out to her, she enrolled at the Toronto International Academy of Design. When asked about her experience there, Alana says, "I know that some people have been very successful with little formal training, but I would never pass up what I learned at the Academy-not to mention, that's where I met my partner, Diana. Developing a strong network of contacts in this industry is very important."

When Alana left school she almost immediately formed, 'Alana Berry,' her own fashion company and label. She has teamed up with one of her former Academy classmates, Diana Calma and is designing elegant custom-tailored formal wear for her clients. Alana believes owning your own company can be very rewarding if you're prepared for "long hours and hard work!"

Instead of immediately heading out on his own, Alex Labayen decided to apprentice with one of Canada's hottest new labels, 'Misura by Joeffer Caoc'. By the way, keep your eye on Joeffer as he has already won the Canadian Designer of the Year award three times, including 1999.

Alex feels that becoming an intern has been a valuable stepping stone to one day going out on his own. His experiences at Misura have already taught him some of the subtler aspects of fashion, "You have to remember it's not for you, the clothes I mean, you just can't design what you like—you have to adapt to what other people want."

Alex has realized that, "People have reasons why they purchase what they do. You have to know what makes people tick, what influences their choices, you really have to learn how to observe what is happening around you and be aware of the past and develop your own ideas of the future."

Working as an apprentice has become an extension of school. Alex says, "I have fun, but it's long hours and hard work (sounds familiar). I've been able to learn about the business side of the industry, things like production, distribution, custom laws, sourcing and marketing. I think this is a great route I've taken because I can learn from someone else's mistakes, learn the ropes, make great contacts and eventually go out on my own better prepared than ever."

***Job Prospects & Career Options of Fashion Designing:*** India which has always been a centre for the textile and garment trade is also growing into a centre of innovation in garment and accessory design. Fashion technology has a wide scope for choosing a career. Now the fashion industry has become so specialized that it encompasses a vast field of studies in design, concept management, design production management, quality control, planning, fabric design, printing, fashion accessory design, fashion merchandising, textile science, colour mixing, marketing and so on.

The primary areas of work in the fashion industry are market research, designing and manufacturing of garments and textiles.

Fashion design is the most important area of work in fashion industry. Designing involves creating original designs after studying the changing trends of the market *i.e.* market research. It has various fields of specialisation like garments, footwear, jewellery and even luggage. It is a challenging field as it requires the coordination of various jobs, in small concerns it is usually a one man show but in big organisations the jobs are specialised and allotted to different people.

Manufacturing involves purchasing textiles and fabrics required for the design and making the garment according to the master pattern. Manufacturing process requires employment of a large number of trained personnel.

***Eligibility:*** Minimum eligibility for the Undergraduate course in this field is 10+2 with 50% marks and for Post Graduate courses graduation.

***Job Prospects and Career Options:*** The candidates after successful completion of the course can find excellent placements in garment, leather and jewellery industry as merchandising executives, fashion designers, illustrators, fashion co-coordinators, etc.

***Remuneration:*** The best bet for a beginner is to get associated with an established designer or design house and begin with doing the menial work.

### *Eligibility & Course Areas*

Minimum eligibility for the Undergraduate course in this field is 10+2 with 50% marks and for Post Graduate courses graduation. In the prominent institutes, admission is strictly on merit- through written test, situation test, group discussion and interview. These courses are aimed at understanding concepts related to costume, jewellery, leather goods and many other similar products where fashion matters.

The courses include Graduate, Post graduate, Certificate and Diploma in the following areas:

1. Accessory designing and fashion designing
2. Garment Manufacturing Technology
3. Apparel marketing and Merchandising
4. Leather and Garment Design and Technology
5. Knitwear Design and Technology
6. Textile Design and Development
7. Fashion Journalism and Presentation

While 10+2 is sufficient for Accessory designing and Fashion Designing, Graduates are preferred for other courses.

The training also includes internship in an organization which gives the students industry functions. Training is usually imparted keeping in mind the demands of the international market. Most training institutes have the latest technologies including laboratories, workshops, design and research centres, libraries, computers and information about the latest development in the industry.

Prominent institutes in Fashion Technology are National institute of Fashion technology (NIFT), National Institute of Design (NID), International Institute of Fashion Technology, New Delhi (IIFT); IEC School of Art and Fashion, New Delhi;

Indian Institute of Art and Fashion Technology (IIAFT), Mumbai; Pearl Academy of fashion, New Delhi; .D. Institute of fashion Technology, New Delhi.

### *Eligibility & Course Areas*

Minimum eligibility for the Undergraduate course in this field is 10+2 with 50% marks and for Post Graduate courses graduation. In the prominent institutes, admission is strictly on merit- through written test, situation test, group discussion and interview. These courses are aimed at understanding concepts related to costume, jewellery, leather goods and many other similar products where fashion matters.

The courses include Graduate, Post graduate, Certificate and Diploma in the following areas:

1. Accessory designing and fashion designing
2. Garment Manufacturing Technology
3. Apparel marketing and Merchandising
4. Leather and Garment Design and Technology
5. Knitwear Design and Technology
6. Textile Design and Development
7. Fashion Journalism and Presentation

While 10+2 is sufficient for Accessory designing and Fashion Designing, Graduates are preferred for other courses.

The training also includes internship in an organization which gives the students industry functions. Training is usually imparted keeping in mind the demands of the international market. Most training institutes have the latest technologies including laboratories, workshops, design and research centres, libraries, computers and information about the latest development in the industry.

Prominent institutes in Fashion Technology are National institute of Fashion technology (NIFT), National Institute of Design (NID), International Institute of Fashion Technology, New Delhi (IIFT); IEC School of Art and Fashion, New Delhi; Indian Institute of Art and Fashion Technology (IIAFT), Mumbai; Pearl Academy of fashion, New Delhi; J.D. Institute of fashion Technology, New Delhi.

***Job Prospects:*** The candidates after successful completion of the course can find excellent placements in garment, leather and jewellery industry as merchandising executives, fashion designers, illustrators, fashion co-coordinators, etc. Export houses, textile mills, garment store chains, boutiques, leather companies, jewellery houses, fashion show organisers also look for such candidates.

### *Fashion Designing is a Lucrative Career*

Fashion designing is the hippest profession today. But no gains without pains, especially with intense competition around. Fashion designing is a lucrative career but one needs to work very hard to keep up with the demand and competitive people. Late nights, continuous hours of work, rejection, disappointment, it's all a part and parcel of the fashion world. Be prepared and take the plunge! What exactly is the profile of a fashion designer? Simply put, it means to make a person look good through his or her clothes. A fashion designer visualizes, plans and implements a dress or attire including its fabric, texture, colour code, accessories etc. To have a career in fashion designing, a person needs to have artistic talents.

Many other skills are important and needed for this kind of major such as being able to work with new materials and information to get involved; skills in analyzing needs and product requirements to create designs; adapting one self in with other people and places. Fashion designers create clothing and accessory designs.

They sketch their original ideas and sometime they even make patterns as guides for cutting samples. Designers are responsible for selecting fabrics, trimmings, a current update on the latest fabrics and fitting the finished clothing to its proper size. To keep current updates on fashion trends, fashion designers often read fashion literature, trade publications and newspapers.

Furthermore, designers will have to be able to combine basic principles of dressmaking and tailoring with flat pattern and draping techniques to get the effect they would want for the clothing. One thing a designer does is to compare their merchandise with the competitors to know what they should do to increase their profits and so on. To start a career as a fashion designer, two types of qualifications are required *i.e.* natural and acquired. Natural skill set would comprise of a decent aesthetic sense, colour coding expertise, good taste and sense of trends and fashion etc.

A designer is like a mentor to his or her client and is expected to figure out the customers' taste, comfort level and preferences. An eye for detail, knowledge of fabrics etc. are also a big plus for those serious about a career as a fashion designer. The acquired skills would be a qualification from a decent, recognized fashion Institute. One can enrol for either a full-time course or a part time certificate course. Not that the courses are not available for graduates or higher qualified people.

There are several short-term certificate courses as well offered by the same Institutes for super specialization, on part-time basis. To be a full pledged professional designer you have to knock the door of some of the Fashion Design Institutes of the country. A good institute will ensure that along with the requisite theoretical inputs, you also get adequate practical exposure to the entire gamut of processes right from formation of textiles and fabric to the most elaborate design elements. Recently several Institutes have started giving training of several kinds, like Merchandising, Knitwear Design & Technology, Apparel Manufacturing, Marketing and Merchandizing.

These Institutes are using world standard curriculum and methodology to build up sharp designers in the demanding Garments & Textile Sector home and abroad. Persons already working in the Garments/Textile Sector/Buying House/RMG Factories can attend these courses to develop their career. Fresher also, to become an expert in the Sector can attend these courses. NIFD (National Institute Of Fashion Design) is a trend setting institute known as "The Cradle of Designers" among the glamour world. It is for those who dream of joining the fascinating fashionable world and for those who wish to become fashionable themselves.

One will learn the basics of fashion and train to develop his/her own spirit of a designer, with a view of the world and the designer collection. Fashion design course prepares you for careers in merchandising fashion, coordination, client servicing, marketing and many more fields. NIFD promises to make its students real professionals having an integrated personality. Besides, you will learn how to make yourself known and to make a living. At NIFD, you will learn not just the art of design, but also the art of being a professional.

### *Career Potential*

Fashion designers work for apparel manufacturers, designing clothing for men, women and children. Some designers cater to specialty stores or large department stores, which may sell a fashion line under a person's name or a company label. Other designers specialize in one aspect of apparel, such as evening gowns or sportswear. A few fashion designers create exclusive, trend-setting fashions that appear on New York and Paris runways, but these designers are the exception rather than the rule.

A concentration in fashion design at the University of North Texas prepares you for a career as a fashion designer or illustrator, or for design and production positions in the fashion industry. A bachelor's degree qualifies you for most jobs in the industry, but teaching fashion design at the college level requires a master of fine arts degree.

UNT's Career Center can help you prepare to pursue your career. The center has information about jobs and employers and the staff can help you with resume and letter writing, job search strategies and interview preparation.

The UNT School of Visual Arts is one of the nation's largest art programmes at a public institution and is considered one of the best in the Southwest. UNT offers a bachelor of fine arts degree with a major in design and a concentration in fashion design.

To enter the fashion design programme, you must complete Design I and II, Drawing I and II and Art Appreciation and then submit a five-piece portfolio containing examples of two-dimensional design, your drawing skills and a special assignment project. The entry portfolio review is once a year and explained in detail in the UNT catalogue. At the end of your second year in the programme, the fashion design faculty will review your portfolio to determine if you can continue in the programme. You also must submit your work in a senior exit review.

As a fashion design student, you will take courses in art history, fashion design, fashion drawing, the history of fashion, industrial sewing techniques and the merchandising/marketing area to learn about fashion retailing.

UNT fashion students have access to the Texas Fashion Collection, which contains 13,000 garments and accessories from the 19th and 20th centuries. Its director, who is also a fashion design faculty member, is nationally recognized as an expert on fashion design and the history of fashion.

As a student, you will be trained in the skills necessary to create original garments and when you graduate, you will have a professional portfolio.

While in school, you will be encouraged to enter national and international competitions. UNT students have successfully competed in the Air France, FOCREA of Belgium, Bobbin World, Natural Fibres and Career Day exhibitions.

Senior students enter a juried exhibition — called ArtWear— held on campus each May. The Dallas-Fort Worth region's leading fashion executives and designers judge this professional runway show.

Getting hands-on experience

Dallas and Fort Worth fashion houses regularly seek interns from UNT. Junior and senior students may be approved for placement in the School of Visual Arts internship programme, in which students earn college credit while working with practicing professionals in the industry.

***Preparing for UNT:*** If you are a high school student, we suggest you prepare for college by becoming computer proficient and taking:

- English ...................... 4 years

- Math .......................... 4 years
- Social science–economics, geography, government, history 4 years
- Science ....................... 3 years
- Foreign language...... 3 years
- Fine arts.................... 1 year

You will need to take courses in most of these subjects under the university core curriculum required of all undergraduates, in addition to your major courses. Talk with your high school counsellor about preparing for college, including the entrance exams (SAT I or ACT) that you should take during your junior year.

As a benefit for transfer students, UNT participates in the Texas Common Course Numbering System. This system makes it easier to transfer credits for general academic courses from one Texas institution to another.

If you're attending a Texas community college, you should consult the UNT Transfer Guide, the UNT Undergraduate Catalogue and an academic counsellor to discuss your degree plan. Proper planning will help you receive the maximum amount of transfer credits.

### *Project Runway*

The hit reality TV show "Project Runway" has drawn attention to careers in fashion design. But the show doesn't reveal all there is to know about fashion careers. Here's what you can and can't learn about life in the fashion fast lane from Heidi Klum and her counterparts.

Watching Project Runway is a great way to learn a little more about the fashion industry and a variety of careers in fashion. You can learn what fashion editors do, how clothing is critiqued and how clothes transform from rough sketches to wearable pieces.

You may also get a better idea of what it's like to feature a collection in a runway show-including what happens minutes before a model walks down the runway, from completing last minute fittings to coordinating hair and makeup that complements a model's overall look. What you may not see much of is how designers actually ply their trade. How did the more skilled illustrators get so good? And how do designers come up with pieces that fit together in an interesting way, one that hints at tradition while pushing toward something more modern and daring?

## Fashion Design Tasks

***School Spotlight:*** The International Academy of Design & Technology is committed to providing academic excellence to help you excel in your chosen career. We can help you turn your natural talent into the kind of skills that could get you a great job in fashion design.

A fashion design job has many aspects. Designers may be responsible for a number of tasks, including researching fashion trends and staying current on contemporary styles; creating sketches and prototypes; choosing materials; going to fashion shows; performing business administration tasks; marketing products; and supervising or working with design team members.

***Skills Needed:*** No fashion designer can get by without creativity and style. The fashion industry is in a constant state of metamorphosis. Fashion designers need to be on their toes. They need to be able to look at old styles and see a new direction to take with their designs. They need to be able to innovate and put a fresh spin on things. From sketching to execution, fashion designers need artistic ability and originality to succeed in the industry.

Setting trends isn't a simple business. Fashion designers have to stay a step ahead. To do that, they need knowledge about previous styles and movements in fashion history. They also need to be aware of current fashion events and developments.

Knowing the ins and outs of business is also beneficial for fashion designers. In this highly competitive industry, aspiring designers can't rely on their artistic vision alone to bring success. For fashion designers, understanding basic principles of marketing and business can help them reach their goals.

A fashion design career isn't for the faint of heart. Fashion designers should be able to work well under pressure. Working with an assortment of people and personalities to meet tight deadlines can be stressful. Those entering this occupation should be willing to work in a team and they should thrive under the demands of deadlines. They should also be able to handle criticism. Critics in this field can be brutal. Successful fashion designers know how to learn from a critique while maintaining their individual style.

### *Is a Fashion Designer Career for You?*

As a fashion designer, you will live on the cutting edge of style. This can be challenging, but if you have the desire and the drive, it can also be fulfilling. Translating your love of fashion design into a career will depend on your talent and, perhaps even more, on your determination to succeed.

### *What is Fashion Merchandising All About?*

Every great boutique or department store needs a Wizard of Oz—someone behind the curtain making everything appear as impressive as possible—someone deciding to stock ruby slippers because they're the next big thing. Fashion merchandising experts accomplish tasks like these on a regular basis.

Fashion merchandising requires a blend of fashion sense and business expertise. Style alone won't yield a successful career in this field. Staying ahead of the fashion curve is a feat involving both art and science. Strategy and marketing know-how are an integral part of fashion merchandising.

### *Fashion Merchandising Tasks*

As a fashion merchandiser, your job is to connect fashion with consumers. To reach that goal, you may do a variety of tasks, including the following:

- Attending fashion shows
- Buying fashions
- Negotiating with suppliers and manufacturers
- Managing retail outlets

- Setting up store displays
- Advertising and marketing

### *Skills Needed*

***School Spotlight:*** AIU offers highly marketable associate's, bachelor's and master's degree programmes in career paths that are technically-oriented and in demand.

While more methodical than fortune telling, fashion merchandising does require forecasting ability. A thorough knowledge of past fashion trends and an awareness of current industry developments will serve you well in a fashion merchandising career.

Problem solving and analytical ability also come in handy in this field. A good sense of style obviously helps you; however, you must also determine how things fit into a budget and whether they meet the functional needs of consumers. Other criteria may also influence your fashion merchandising decisions, so you will need to be able to analyze a complex set of issues and stand behind your choices.

Fashion merchandising also requires good communication skills. From negotiating with manufacturers to getting your marketing message out to customers, there is ample opportunity to exercise your powers of communication in the fashion merchandising field.

*Is Fashion Merchandising for You?*

A job in this field will put you at the intersection of fashion and business. If you have a head for business and an eye for style, a fashion merchandising career may be just the right fit for you.

## Design Training: Guide to Selected Schools

Gaining recognition as a professional designer is a ticket to opportunity and the right design school is therefore key. The career choices available to creative individuals who have received proper training are almost limitless.

Whether your goal is a career in design, or is one of self-improvement for your own pleasure, you can fulfil your dreams at any one of many design training centres across the United States and Canada. This site aims to help put you in the picture.

These design training centres offer a wide range of opportunity to develop skills and careers in 3-D Design, Advertising, Animation, Computer Graphics, Desktop Publishing, Digital Design and Imaging, Fashion Design, Illustration, Digital Video, Interior Design and Decoration, Typography, Multimedia, Photography, Photo styling, Textile Arts, User Interface Design, Online Publishing, Web Design, Web Application Development and CAD Design.

### *A Career in Fashion Design*

The fashion design career, has recently emerged as one of the most popular and competitive among young people. Those who actually succeed in design have a very individualistic personal style and don't follow trends set by others. Having fashion design as your profession sometimes allows you to meet glamorous people. It can also put you in charge of what is in and out when it comes to clothing through ramp shows and fashion write-ups. Most designers have a great social status and are accepted by everyone. However, There are many aspects which may or may not help you choose it as your career.

Many talented individuals are attracted to careers as designers. Those with little or no education, as well as those who lack perseverance, will find it difficult to establish and maintain a career in fashion design. There were over 16,000 people employed in this field in 2003 and demand will stay strong for designers because of our cons.

### *Art, Design & Fashion*

It is possible to design the career of your dreams, especially when crafty and creative are often used to describe your talents. The fields of art and design and fashion are like an empty canvas, brimming with endless possibilities and art and design schools and fashion programmes can provide you with the right tools for creating your career masterpiece. Whether your interests like in graphic art and design, Web design, photography, fashion design, computer animation, or interior design, you can choose from a wide field of programmes and degrees. Add colour to your career by researching art and design schools.

### *Computer Animation*

Have an eye for design and a taste for tech? Then consider a degree in computer animation. What used to be a simple field has expanded into an industry with stakes in movies, video games, TV and web design. Whether it's Disney and Pixar's "Cars" or the latest game from Blizzard, computer animation is at the forefront of new media.

And with more colleges and universities offering certificates and degrees in computer animation, the variety of specialized courses has also gone on the rise—helping to boost students' credentials in the process. That's because computer animation isn't just about moving characters or realistic polygons, anymore; it's about telling a story in a whole new way. Some degree programmes—such as for video game design—will take computer animation to the next level by offering courses in storytelling in addition to their traditional technical instruction.

It's the perfect combination if you're interested in getting a career in the industry or even starting your own studio. If you're more interested in the technical aspects of computer animation consider a career in special effects. Using computer animation, special effects wizards have made lasers zap in "Star Wars" and fires blaze in "Ghost Rider." So, come on. Why not get your game on with a computer animation degree?

Think a career in fashion design is as simple as sketching a new look? Think again. In this fast-paced and multifaceted industry, the more you know the better your chance of getting hired. While it's true that fashion designers used to live by the pencil and pad, this fabric-focused field has long-since increased its dependency on Silicon Valley.

***Translation:*** you'll need to know your way around a keyboard to succeed. Though you'll deal with plenty of hands-on cutting and sewing, many fashion designers today rely on computer programmes to design and share their new looks. Gaining an understanding of the programmes that shape the field will increase your marketability as well as visibility. But no matter how good of an artist or designer you are, you'll need more than a stellar portfolio to survive—you'll need to understand this competitive field. Fashion design schools can help you by offering courses not only in computers, but in the legal and business aspects of the fashion design industry as well.

After all, what's the point of coming up with a killer new-look if you can't market or protect your idea? If you want a successful career in fashion design, think about more than just colours and shapes and get a degree from a fashion design school.

### *Advertising & Design*

Take your creativity to a new level by exploring advertising and design training that will help you market yourself. With the right combination of technical skills, design savvy and an eye for business, you can be part of creative teams that develop award-winning advertising in print, online and in other multimedia outlets.

Advertising and design involves developing creative elements like branding, logos, images, company literature, flash presentations and other advertising materials that help make a client's products and services recognizable to the consumer. By taking coursework in advertising and design, you will learn your way around industry graphic design and Web design programmes; basic art and business skills; and lots more.

Those who take advertising and design courses via an art school or specialized art programme will focus more heavily on the design aspects of the field, as opposed to someone who follows an advertising and design track as part of a business degree (for which classes will include general business areas like finance and management).

Whichever route you choose to launch your advertising and design career, be sure to take advantage of internship opportunities to gain hands-on experience in the field. It will help you to develop a portfolio of work when competing for jobs in advertising and design.

***Reviewing Fashion Trends can Help Make you a Top Designer***

Lila Rivera always dreamed of being a fashion designer. "I just grew up with it and learned a lot from my mom," said Rivera, a graduate of the Art Institute of Fort Lauderdale and owner of Amaya Swimwear. "My first job out of school was on a photo shoot. While working, I met many influential people who guided me in the industry. I would advise anyone who wants to work as a fashion designer to try and work as many jobs as possible so you can get your name out there and build your reputation. Through hard work and networking, I eventually started my own line of swimwear."

Fashion designers help create clothing, shoes and accessories that are purchased by consumers. Designers study fashion trends, sketch designs of clothing and accessories and sell and oversee the final production of their designs. Clothing designers create and help produce apparel, such as casual wear, suits, sportswear and formal wear. Careers in fashion also include shoe designers, who create and produce different styles of shoes and boots and accessory designers, who design items that add the finishing touches to an outfit, such as handbags, belts, scarves, hats and hosiery. Some fashion designers even specialize in costume design for performing arts, motion pictures or television.

Andre West, chairman of the Fashion Design Department at the Art Institute of Fort Lauderdale, said creativity, being in tune with the fashion industry and staying flexible are some of the keys to success. "Go to school and learn as much as you can from those already in the field," West advised. "Most students think they can go into business for themselves right after school and that just isn't the case. You must allow yourself to learn from other designers as you begin your career." Beginning fashion designers usually start out as pattern makers or sketching assistants before they can advance to higher-level positions.

Some designers may start their own design companies, or design fashions for their own retail stores or boutiques. Employers usually seek individuals with a two- or four-year degree. They also look for designers who have a strong sense of the esthetics of fashion, details, a sense of balance and proportion and an appreciation for beauty. A good portfolio, which contains a collection of patterns and designs, also is important in finding a job.

"An associate degree in fashion design usually takes 18 months to two years," West said. "A bachelor's degree will take about three years and will help you develop your style and skill levels. Once you obtain your degree, internships are a good place to begin so you can get your foot in the door and learn about the business. Getting a job in retail also is important so you can learn about consumers, their tastes and demographics. You need to focus your designs for the market you are catering to."

The fashion programme at the Art Institute of Fort Lauderdale instructs students to develop their skills in design and pattern making. Students learn both traditional and computer-generated designs, as well as developing their own sense of design and style.

"In addition to creativity and sketching ability, fashion designers also need to have sewing and computer skills and the ability to understand how garments should be constructed," West said. "Fashion designers also need excellent presentation skills in order to persuade clients to purchase their designs. Good teamwork and personality are necessary because of the increasingly international nature of the business that requires designers to be in contact with suppliers, manufacturers and buyers around the world."

Salaries for fashion designers can vary widely based on the employer and years of experience. Average salaries range from $38,000 to $100,000 a year and up for top designers.

Some high schools offer fashion programmes to allow students the opportunity to try their hand at fashion design before entering a college programme. One such programme is the Fashion Design Academy at Santaluces High School in Boynton Beach. Michelle Matella has been the director of the fashion programme at Santaluces for the last six years.

"Our fashion design academy teaches design techniques for construction and patterns, along with other hands-on skills that lay the groundwork for a career in fashion design," Matella said. "They learn the basics of fashion design in our level-one class and then can complete levels two through five if they choose to continue in the programme.

The highlight for students who enter the fashion programme is our annual fashion show at the end of the school year. The show highlights each student's fashions and they also model their creations. It is a big draw for our programme."

"You must really love this career," Matella said. "It can be an extremely challenging field to work in. I would advise anyone to explore all the job opportunities out there in the fashion industry to find the career that best suites your interests."

### *Fashion Design Schools*

Start a career in fashion design and be creative all day long. The Fashion Designing industry is a fast-paced, competitive and ever-changing field. Hard work, determination and a creative and technical mind-set, as well as the constant passion to keep yourself focused each day, are needed to succeed in this field.

Successful fashion designers must understand and be adaptable to all the changes and challenges of the fashion industry. They must have the ability to visually present their ideas and to actually produce them.

There are many job opportunities in the world of fashion design, make sure you pick a school and programme that provides the right kind of training for you to advance in your fashion career.

## Charting your Path with Academic Advising

You must attend an orientation to the School of Visual Arts, which is held at approximately the same time as university orientation for new students or during registration at the start of each semester. Check with the university admissions office for a schedule of freshman and transfer student orientations.

## Fashion Design & Merchandising

In the exciting field of Fashion Design and Merchandising, you can turn your talent for fashion into a career you love. Study Fashion Design & Merchandising at Katharine Gibbs School New York and let your love for the business of fashion lead toward exciting career opportunities.

The Fashion Design & Merchandising Associate in Applied Science is designed to prepare students to work in almost any facet of the fashion industry. Students at Gibbs School can learn to integrate conceptual and creative abilities with technical and professional business practices, while they have the opportunity to master both the requirements of design as well as the requirements of marketing to the ultimate customer.

Here are some of the best things about the Fashion Design & Merchandising specialized degree programme:

- Training in creative design, technical design, marketing, merchandising and visual merchandising
- Opportunities to stage fashion shows offer real-life industry experience
- Focused instruction by professionals in the industry
- A curriculum designed to provide knowledge and skill in all aspects of sales and promotion as well as broad-based career courses
- Programme completion in as few as 18 months helps get you working sooner than you think in a career you love
- Final quarter internships allow students to work with professionals in an established fashion company
- Courses that allow students to focus on their creative talents

Fashion Design and Marketing & Graphic Design Classes Begin Soon in San Antonio

Registration is open at the International Academy of Design & Technology—San Antonio, offering new classes for students looking to explore exciting career opportunities.

San Antonio, TX (PRWEB) April 16, 2007—The International Academy of Design & Technology in San Antonio opened its doors on April 2, 2007, offering students a chance to explore opportunities in two of today's hot career fields: fashion design and marketing & graphic design.

IADT—San Antonio is part of a network of IADT schools in North America, offering diploma and degree programmes in a wide range of areas. IADT also has campuses in Chicago, Detroit, Las Vegas, Nashville, Orlando, Pittsburgh, Schaumburg, Seattle, Tampa and Toronto.

Students who want to learn the fundamentals of fashion design and marketing while cultivating their individual creativity can register for the Fashion Design and Marketing diploma programme. The school's creative training facility offers hands-on, skill-building classes for preparation in today's global marketplace. Students can also learn effective marketing techniques for advertising their unique creations.

The Graphic Design diploma programme can help students develop their artistic abilities and build the foundation necessary for success in the graphic design field. Students can learn practical applications of graphic design in a dynamic learning environment.

***Associate of Arts Degree:*** Are you driven by a lifelong love of fashion? Does the idea of designing clothing for a living make you think "dream job"?

If fashion is your favourite way to express yourself, the fashion design programme at Brooks College—Long Beach can help you gain the skills you need to become an inspired member of the fashion industry. Our intense 18-month programme offers a quality all-around education in both the creative and business aspects of this exciting career field.

As a fashion design student, you can cultivate your creativity while having the opportunity to learn the fundamentals of design. You'll also explore the different marketing techniques that can dramatically affect fashion sales. Our fashion design faculty consists of established designers, marketers and merchandisers who can provide in-depth instruction, giving you an opportunity to gain a solid foundation in everything from advertising and retailing to design principles, illustration, custom patterns and fashion show production.

Areas of focus include:

- Fashion illustration
- Design techniques
- Fashion design software
- Business skills
- Marketing and consumer behaviour
- Fashion show production and promotion

Graduates of our Fashion Design Programme should be qualified to address any design challenge, as well as any situation that requires solid business sensibilities. Build a professional portfolio and prepare for career opportunities as a:

- Fashion designer
- Design assistant
- Alteration specialist
- Fashion Illustrator
- Production assistant

Are you ready for the world of fashion design? Is the world of fashion design ready for you? Contact Brooks College today for a quality choice of Fashion Design Programmes in California!

Be sure to check out these other related programmes offered at Brooks College in Long Beach:

- *Fashion Merchandising:* This programme teaches the business side of the industry and can help prepare you for an exciting career in fashion merchandising.
- *Interior Design:* Apply your sense of style and design to internal spaces and train for an exciting career in interior design.

### *Your Career in the Fashion Industry*

Connecting Fashion Career Candidates with Employers and Recruiters

"Fashion is in the sky, in the street, fashion has to do with ideas, the way we live, what is happening", said Coco Chanel, legendary fashionista. Fashion design jobs today are vibrant and fast-paced, always at the forefront of popular culture. Fashion design careers intersect with music, the silver screen, art and interior design. .Style is everywhere and fashion designers are responsible for shaping it.

The fashion industry as we know it today began with Charles Frederick Worth, the Father of Haute Couture, who established the first fashion house in 1858. A generation later the fashion industry took off, with seminal designers Lanvin, Chanel, Balenciaga and Dior dominating the scene. It was during this time that designers became artists, as their jobs shifted from actually sewing a garment to sketching or painting designs.

Paris remained the center for fashion design jobs until World War II, when the focus shifted to New York and Hollywood. This was the era of the celebrity fashion icon, a trend that lasted into the sixties with glamour queens like Grace Kelly and Audrey Hepburn. Meanwhile, street fashion and unusual textiles inspired the careers of British designers Vivienne Westwood and Betsey Johnson. Fashion began to favour a hip, young market—a departure from the grand old haute couture.

Today, ready-to-wear fashion dominates the industry. Ready-to-wear designer lines offer high quality workmanship and trendsetting styles. As new high-tech fabrics emerge, textile careers are gaining popularity. A contemporary fashion design career is an applied art, as much about defining lifestyles as clothing.

Fashion and textile careers range from design er to stylist, sewer to wardrobe consultant. It's the fashion designer's job to create new looks and set trends. Pattern-makers and sample makers are responsible for bringing these new designs to life. A fashion stylist's job is to interpret these bold designs for a general market. Fashion merchandisers watch trends and market new designs and buyers assemble a collection for retail, attending shows and placing orders with manufacturers.

A fashion design career is a labour of love for many and competition for the best positions can be fierce. A strong fashion resume features a college degree, internships and a portfolio. Education is crucial—the standard qualification is either a 2-year associate or 4-year bachelor of fine arts degree.

Coursework includes colour, textiles, sewing and tailoring, pattern-making, fashion merchandising and computer-aided design (CAD). In addition to internships, contests offer valuable exposure and can really make a fashion resume stand out.

The median annual income for fashion and textile design careers was $55,840 in 2004. Salaries vary widely based on experience and employer— fashion designers can earn anywhere from $27,970 to $112,840. It's a labour of love, but with determination, talent and a winning fashion resume, you can establish a design career and start making fashion history.

***Fashion Designer***

***The Work:*** Fashion designers can choose to work in one of three different areas – high fashion (known as 'haute couture'), designer ready-to-wear and high-street fashion. Within these areas there is often the opportunity to specialise further, for example into men's, children's or sportswear.

The work of fashion designers varies from company to company, but typically involves:

- working to a design brief
- analysing or predicting trends in fabrics, colours and shapes
- producing concept and mood boards
- developing blocks (basic shapes) through patterns
- estimating costs for materials and manufacture
- finding suppliers
- supervising the making up of sample garments
- making in-house presentations, for example to finance departments and merchandisers.

Fashion designers often work closely with garment technologists and sample machinists. They also liaise with manufacturers (often based overseas) to ensure that designs are reproduced accurately.

***Hours and Environment:*** As a fashion designer you will often work long hours and weekends in order to meet deadlines– for example the launch of a new collection. You will probably find that you never 'switch off' as you will always be looking for inspiration.

You will usually work in a studio or workshop, but will have opportunities to travel to visit manufacturers (often overseas) or for research visits, for example to art galleries, trade shows or to particular places or countries that are linked to a design theme.

***Skills and Interests:*** To be a fashion designer you need:

- a good eye for colour, texture and shape
- an understanding of the properties of fabrics and how they can be used
- technical skills such as pattern cutting and sewing
- the ability to spot and develop trends
- drawing skills
- the ability to use computer aided design (CAD)
- understanding of production processes
- the ability to solve problems
- commercial awareness
- the ability to work as part of a team.

***Entry:*** To become a fashion designer you will usually need a relevant degree. A degree that teaches both design and technical skills will give you the practical knowledge needed to work in the industry.

The following universities offer relevant courses:

- Manchester Metropolitan University
- London College of Fashion
- De Montfort University, Leicester
- Heriot Watt University, Edinburgh
- University of Manchester.

You can also do degrees in fashion design at other UK higher education institutions. To search for colleges and universities offering fashion & textile-related courses and degrees, visit the website of the Universities and Colleges Admissions Service (UCAS). Please check with the individual colleges and universities for their entry requirements.

You will need to put together a portfolio of work that you can take along to interviews, which should include mood-boards, designs and technical drawings. It is also important to take along actual garments you have produced.

Because the industry is very competitive (more than 3,000 fashion and textiles students qualify from higher education each year), any work experience you gain will give you an advantage when it comes to getting a job.

***Training:*** You will usually enter the industry as a design assistant before working up to be a designer - practical experience in the job and a good track record are therefore crucial to progressing in your career.

You can develop your knowledge and skills by attending short courses and masterclasses. For example, London College of Fashion offers a range of courses covering aspects of design and related technical skills.

Postgraduate degrees and diplomas in specialised areas of fashion design and related subjects are available. You will usually need relevant first degree before doing one of these.

You can gain professional recognition by joining the Textile Institute (TI) and applying for qualifications on three levels: Licentiate, Associate and Fellow. To find out more, visit the TI website. The TI also runs conferences, seminars and short courses.

The Design Association Academy offers a Diploma in Design Business Management, which may be relevant if you are self-employed or freelance.

***Opportunities:*** As a fashion designer you will usually work for high street retailers or independent labels.

Once you have developed the skills you need to be a successful fashion designer, you can progress to positions such as senior designer or head of department, for example head of women's wear design, or design director.

Alternatively, you may decide to become a freelance designer (employed by companies on a project-by-project basis), or become self-employed and launch your own collection.

***Annual Income:*** Figures are intended as a guideline only.

The starting salary for a fashion designer can be between £12,000 to £14,000 a year.

With experience and increased responsibility this can increase to £22,000 to £60,000 plus.

***Figures are Higher for London-based Designers***

Freelance designers may charge per design or per collection and rates vary widely. Agents may take up to 30 per cent as commission.

Bachelor of Applied Design in Fashion Design and Technology and Diploma in Fashion Design and Technology

The four-year Bachelor of Applied Design in Fashion Design and Technology degree programme provides a unique integrated study of design, production and marketing which is essential for career success. Students will develop analytical and critical thinking skills, creative problem solving abilities and skills in computers, business, marketing and communications. Comprehensive industry-based training and an extensive internship are featured.

Kwantlen also offers a two-year Fashion Design and Technology Diploma Programme and a one-year Fashion Marketing Certificate Programme.

The four-year selective-entry programme is organized into eight semesters with a minimum of 120 credits in total. The programme may be taken on a part-time or full-time basis. Some limitations apply to part-time studies. The diploma consists of 62.5 credits total.

The focus of the programme is on education and training in areas of design, production and marketing for the apparel industry. A typical fashion career requires awareness of market trends, the ability to design for a specific market and knowledge of pattern drafting, fit, sewing, costing and working with in-house production people or contractors.

Considerable demands are placed on students to develop professional standards in problem solving and technical skills. The programme simulates a professional atmosphere by providing relevant equipment and by demanding punctuality and strict adherence to schedules. Garments designed throughout the programme reflect market trends by balancing creativity with marketability and are produced in standard sizes using industrial drafting and sewing techniques. Students enjoy the opportunity to study and learn about the role of a fashion designer through industry linked classroom projects in collaboration with local apparel companies.

General or liberal education electives, English, marketing, business and communications courses which students will take as part of the degree will expose them to a breadth of study which enriches students as designers. Writing and making presentations are important elements of the programme.

High quality production equipment includes: industrial straight sewing and specialty machines, sergers, steam irons, a vacuum press and a fusing machine. Classrooms are spacious and well lit. State-of-the-art computers and apparel industry software are used for designing, spec drawing, costing, pattern manipulation, grading and marker making.

Certain courses are structured to simulate a workplace or job environment. Others require students to work extensively in groups to meet course objectives. In both these cases, students are expected to attend classes regularly, to be punctual and to demonstrate a satisfactory level of performance and rate of progress within the timelines set for various course activities. The programme includes an extensive internship in the third year.

***Student Profile:*** Most people who apply to the programme have a passionate lifelong interest in fashion. They may come directly from high school, transfer from other institutions, be mature individuals returning to the profession or making a career change, or industry personnel seeking upgrading. Applicants have a desire to undertake the depth of study that a degree programme offers.

Applicants with experience in the fashion industry may gain credits through Prior Learning Assessment (PLA). Graduates from a two-year fashion programme who wish to pursue a degree will be assessed in a flexible manner.

Kwantlen has a student exchange agreement with a fashion school in Helsinki, Finland and is developing further exchange opportunities.

Students may challenge segments of the programme for course work taken elsewhere and gain advanced standing at various levels.

Industry personnel who wish to take specific courses or courses on a part-time basis to complement their job skills may do so with permission of the Programme Coordinator. Application deadlines to the programme and English language entrance requirements apply. Some course prerequisites may be waived based on work experience. Contact the Programme Coordinator for further information.

***Career Opportunities:*** The apparel industry, important in being the fifth largest secondary industry in B.C., is changing to compete with global and domestic markets.

With over 300 apparel companies in the lower mainland, BC has a well-established apparel industry. Graduates work for vibrant lower mainland companies such as Mac& Jac, Sugoi, Mavi Jeans, Off—The-Wall, Dish Clothing and Flosport. Depending upon capabilities and interests, students work for large companies as members of design, production or marketing teams, for smaller design houses where they are expected to work in all aspects of the business, or engage in entrepreneurial or freelance endeavours.

Retail management is another option. Similar opportunities are available worldwide. In all instances, graduates need to be well versed in all three areas (design, production and marketing) of the business to participate fully as team players. Emerging designers prosper best if they have a solid background and experience in production and marketing.

Kwantlen has an agreement with UBC whereby Fashion students interested in a career as a high school clothing and textiles teacher may be eligible for entry to UBC's Bachelor of Education programme in Home Economics upon completion of Kwantlen's fashion degree, including 6 credits in English and 18 credits in Family Studies courses. Family Studies courses may be taken at UBC as either a visiting student at UBC while completing Kwantlen's fashion programme (Family Studies courses can be used as elective credit for Kwantlen's fashion degree) or as a UBC student following graduation from Kwantlen's fashion programme.

The programme offers a successful informal job placement service due to its ties to industry.

### *Fashion Design Degree at IADT Schaumburg*

Have you always dreamed of an exciting fashion career? Always wanted to learn more about the art of fashion design? Make that dream a reality with the fashion design degree programme at IADT—Schaumburg.

### *Prepare For Your Career in Fashion Design*

The fashion design training at IADT Schaumburg is designed to keep pace with the rapid changes in the global fashion industry. You will have the opportunity to learn the various facets of the fashion designing industry in this exciting programme.

While earning your Fashion Design Degree, you'll study a combination of traditional fashion designing techniques as well as computer-based design, pattern drafting and manufacturing. At the International Academy of Design and Technology, our fashion design training is continually updated to stay current with the latest innovations in the field.

### *Benefits of Earning a Degree in Fashion Design*

The fashion design degree programme can benefit all students seeking a fashion career—from novices to established professionals. Our graduates are well-rounded fashion designers with both conventional and innovative design skills.

Our fashion design training can teach you the technology behind industry-current design techniques. Such modern skills can give you an edge in the ultra-competitive fashion design industry. Our students want more than just a job. They're looking for successful fashion careers. Feel the same way? Then IADT's fashion design degree programme is for you!

### *Fashion School: Filling the Gaps*

Of course a TV show can't provide us with a thorough education in fashion design or anything else. To learn about the ins and outs of the fashion industry and clothing design from pattern-making to clothing construction, you need to attend fashion school. Fashion school can equip you with the fundamental knowledge needed to begin practicing your passion-you may even begin developing some level of expertise during your academic career, building a portfolio that could help you land your first post-fashion school job.

Careers in fashion are hard won-and that's one topic that Project Runway depicts realistically. The contestants are typically very talented and the competition is extremely tough. So don't delay your fashion education; you'll need all the preparation and advantages available to pursue your career in fashion.

## Five Myths and Five Tips

For many women, becoming a fashion designer is a lifelong dream. We all love to wear beautiful clothes and make ourselves feel good from the inside out.

We often imagine what it feels like to actually make money doing something this great: dressing people up and making them feel good, models catwalking the runway gracefully to showcase our designs, stylists working frantically at the backstage and we are introduced as "the designer" at the closing. Ah, pretty tempting, indeed, but somehow it feels so surreal. Can I actually become a fashion designer?

Despite the misconception that only those who graduate from New York prestigious fashion schools can make it big in this highly lucrative and competitive field, many fashion designers literally work their way up working from home.

Karen and Warren Hipwell, for instance, started and still operate design studio from their residence in Massachusetts. Despite their humble start, now their products are sold in 110 retailers nationwide. Pure luck? Think again.

You, too, can become a fashion designer even if you have never worn "designer" clothes, don't have a fashion degree, can't draw or sew and live far away from New York or Los Angeles. These are no more than myths. Let me briefly explain them to you.

***Myth One:*** I have never worn "designer" clothes.

***Reality:*** All clothes, including those in your closet, are designed by fashion designers. Many people confuse designer "collection," which means high-priced seasonal line designed by top designers, with "the person" who designs clothes.

***Myth Two:*** I don't have a fashion degree.

***Reality:*** Unlike the medical professions, which require extensive classroom and hands-on training, you can learn how to design anywhere. No special education is needed. You'll be surprised to know that many established designers don't have any special training.

***Myth Three:*** I live far away from New York or Los Angeles.

***Reality:*** While NY and LA are great places to find an internship position with established designers, fashion is a part of life and fashion designers can be found everywhere. Whether you live in a city of millions or a town of 10,000, there must be at least a few local fashion designers.

***Myth Four:*** I cannot draw or sew.

***Reality:*** Nobody can at the beginning. Strong motivation and perseverance are more important than how well you can draw or sew. Such skills can be learned easily (including using some free resources).

***Myth Five:*** I don't feel comfortable working in a high-profile industry.

***Reality:*** Well, this glamorous image is no more than the most over-rated trait of the fashion industry. This image is created by the media with the help of fashion publicists and marketers to boost sales. Thus, the purpose is pure business. The better the coverage, the better the sales will be. Fashion designers work very hard for 18 to 24 months to deliver the best designs of the season.

Now you're ready to plunge into this often-misunderstood field, here are some tips:

First, a fashion designer is an artist and an entrepreneur in one. Why? Because if you design in the name of art without considering the marketability, it's very likely you won't be successful. Many designers fail because of this.

Second, you can choose your design specializations from a long list of classifications. Trivial items, such as beach and leg wears, are highly profitable products and relatively easy to produce compared with haute couture pieces.

Third, understand what your career goal is. You can choose whether you want to work for others or for yourself. Whichever one your choice is, apprenticeship is always a great option for new designers.

Fourth, keep up with the industry trends and news. Travel and read a lot to be informed and inspired. New insights will keep your creative skills fresh and ready to roll.

Fifth, persevere. Perseverance is the most important virtue of all because without it, nothing can be completed. Perseverance is your ticket to the peak of your career.

What is fashion?

In short, it's the clothes we wear. It's also the way we cut our hair. It often dicates what makeup, jewellery, cologne or the shoes we put on in the morning.

At work, it can be tell others how seriously we want to be taken at the office and in social situations fashion can be used as a status symbol telegraphing our worth.

Fashion is not so much who we are, but an important part of what we want to show "our public."

On the Web, check out what else fashion may mean—at top sites chronicling its history, along with news about what's hot right now, fashion trend predictions and the latest cutting edge styles that continually redefine not so much who we are, but how we look...

***Fashion History & Costume History Eras, Victorian to Haute Couture:*** Everything you ever wanted to know about fashion is included in this online illustrated encyclopedia covering the latest trends as well as fashion theory & technology, timelines, a look at important fashion eras, royal & couture fashions, related links & resources.

***NH Extra—Fashion:*** Great intro to the topic at this archived PBS special for students including an, pictures, discussions & interviews on hip-hop fashion, nail colours, student uniforms, hi-tech fabrics and a special look at fast food fashions...

***AskMen.com—Men's Trends:*** Great resource for guys who want to know what's in this season with tips & advice on shoes, cologne, suits, formal & casual wear, trendy watches & jewellery.

***Fashion Windows:*** The latest fashion news headlines, designer bio's, what's hot and in season, plus related resources including online industry forum, classifieds, event calendar.

***Fashion Trends in Japan:*** Trendy, edgy fashions now being seen on the streets of Tokyo and elsewhere, with news & feature articles on what's hot and what's about to be in style in the months ahead.

***Sky.com—Fashion:*** The Euro news organization with the latest gossip, rumors and celebrity fashion news, picture galleries and feature stories.

Fashion Design, Marketing, Merchandising Programmes:

- Fashion Design
- Fashion Design and Marketing
- Fashion Design and Merchandising
- Fashion Marketing and Merchandising
- Fashion Merchandising
- Merchandising Management: Fashion Merchandising

***Fashion Design:*** The International Academy of Design and Technology's programme in Fashion Design is an intense, two-year course of study that can prepare graduates for a career in the designing, making and marketing of fashion.

By the time the graduates are ready to enter the industry, they have started a professional portfolio which can include apparel for men, women and children, as well as accessories.

Fashion Design is available in:

- Chicago, Illinois

- Schaumburg, Illinois
- Detroit, Michigan
- Las Vegas, Nevada
- Seattle, Washington
- Toronto, Canada

***Fashion Design & Marketing:*** International Academy of Design and Technology can prepare you for many exciting careers in fashion styling, including fashion design, fashion illustration, production, costume design, merchandising, textile artistry and pattern drafting.

Fashion Design & Marketing is available in:

- Tampa, Florida
- San Antonio, Texas

***Fashion Design & Merchandising:*** The International Academy's programme in fashion design and merchandising is demanding, technical and comprehensive. Students can learn about fashion illustration, pattern drafting, design, draping, clothing construction, textiles, fashion history, fashion merchandising and production techniques. The fashion design and merchandising programme also focuses on the global fashion and merchandising industry focusing on market and trend research, design development, visual displays, sales and business practices and production management. All of the instruction is presented using industrial grade equipment in spacious and comfortable facilities built for optimum fashion designing.

A balanced curriculum can provide students with the expertise to design and communicate their ideas combining theoretical elements of design with creative and practical approaches to the solution of problems pertaining to the functional quality of marketable products. A foundation in general education coursework rounds out the student's knowledge base.

Fashion Design & Merchandising is available in:

- Orlando, Florida
- Nashville, Tennessee

## Fashion Marketing Programmes

Upon graduating from a fashion marketing school, there are a number of careers open to students who are passionate about the billion-dollar fashion industry. Because many fashion marketing degrees combine classes in fashion design and fashion merchandising, students are often equipped to take on the fashion industry from either the creative or business side.

On the business side, fashion marketing graduates often become fashion buyers, merchandisers, fashion advertising agents, fashion event planners, or importing/exporting agents. Many of today's top designers have actually emerged from this business side instead of starting to design first. This progression is logical, because a successful designer must focus both on what he thinks will be cutting edge in fashion and what people will buy.

A solid foundation in fashion marketing can help a designer understand the needs of her target audience. Those designers who don't come from a marketing background depend on the fashion marketers for advice. Although the job of fashion marketer might not always allow you to put your name on a clothing line, the power you have to sell that clothing line can help line your own pockets rather nicely.

The route taken most often by those emerging as the next class of fashion marketers starts with networking with those that came before them. More acute in the fashion industry than in most other industries, professional relationships account for much of the career success that can be enjoyed.

## Bachelors Degree in Fashion Merchandising

There are three ways to get started in fashion merchandising: earning a four year bachelors degree, a two year associates degree, or working within the fashion industry, learning along the way. Employers are often looking for a candidate who has graduated from a top fashion merchandising school and has developed a portfolio and resume with skilled teachers and industry mentors.

A 4-year bachelors degree is generally more comprehensive than an associates degree and offers classes outside of the professional focus that can help give a student some context into their major field of study. Classes that would be included in a fashion merchandising bachelor degree that would not be included in an associate degree would be art or fashion history, economics, etc. These classes do not specifically prepare a student for fashion merchandising, but give a student a well-rounded background that could help them be better problem-solvers once they enter the workplace, because they'll have a deeper breath of knowledge from which to draw.

## Associate Degrees in Fashion Design

There are three basic ways of getting an education in fashion design: earning a four year bachelors degree, a two year associates degree, or working within the fashion industry, learning along the way. All three methods have been proven to be successful by today's leading fashion designers, but because of today's increasingly competitive fashion design job market, employers are more often looking for a candidate who has graduated from a top fashion design school and has developed a portfolio with skilled teachers.

Although a bachelors degree is generally more comprehensive than an associates degree, the additional education a student receives in a bachelors programme does not necessarily give her more skills to become a better fashion designer. The professional skills needed to begin a career in fashion design such as fabric printing and print design, sketching for a designer and illustrator, industry-standard pattern drafting and showroom/retail sales, for example, are taught at both the associate and bachelor level.

What is lacking in an associate degree are the more liberal art classes, such as art history, which are helpful to add context to the professional classes, but not essential to learning the design trade. Those students who either want to save money on their education or are anxious to get into the professional world may be good candidates for a two-year associate degree. This choice does not necessarily short-change an education, as some students learn better in a professional setting than they do in an academic one.

### *1 and 2-year Fashion Merchandising Diplomas*

While there are many ways to get started in the fashion marketing industry, employers increasingly look for a candidate with a degree from a top fashion merchandising school.

An associate degree typically distills the professional classes needed to enter the fashion merchandising industry from the non-essential classes which help round out a students education. These skills include retail merchandising, fashion basics, speech communication, promotion of fashion, principles of marketing and the principles of selling, for example. Students earning an associates degree instead of a bachelors would forgo more academic classes such as art history, or economics, for example, that could prove to be useful down the road of a professional career.

Because an associate degree is only two years, it proves useful for those who either cannot afford a four-year degree or are anxious to enter the working world. An associate degree education actually proves more useful to some, who learn better in a professional setting than in an academic one. Associate degree students often benefit by the structure and set path of learning the basics of the trade and then gaining most of their working knowledge of the business from professional mentors.

## Fashion Design and Production

The world of fashion is fast-paced and exciting. The Fashion majors at Lasell focus on the specialized areas of retail merchandising, clothing design and visual and promotional design techniques. Other supporting industries such as marketing and advertising are examined through courses in business, textiles, garment design, pattern marking, grading, photography, buying, operations and fashion history. Students use the latest computer-aided design (CAD/CAM) equipment to make production markers and engineer patterns for optimal material use. The degree includes a solid foundation in both liberal arts and business courses. Through Lasell's connected Learning philosophy, students have ongoing opportunities to apply theoretical concepts of academic studies by working in the field with recognized leaders in the fashion industry. The upper-level professional courses are oriented toward decision-making tasks that students will face when making the transition from college to middle and upper management positions. Students learn how to plan strategically, organize for profitability (using design cost sheets and computer costing technology pertinent to each degree), control design operations and promote creativity.

Every Fashion student, in each of the four years, has on and off-site opportunities or contact with industry professionals. These opportunities include professional consultation on academic projects and all Fashion students are involved directly in on- and off-campus fashion show productions as designers, producers, set designers, or stylists. Involvement in professional application projects becomes particularly intensive in the senior year through our Fashion Design capstone courses in Thesis Development and Production or the Internship Seminar and Field Assignment in Fashion Merchandising.

Each student in the Fashion Design major develops an electronic portfolio that documents his or her educational experiences from the first year through graduation.

Our Graduates pursue careers as fashion designers, technical designers, buyers and merchandisers. Our graduates are known for their accomplishments and talent and recognized with awards, high-level job placements and accolades from industry leaders. Graduates receive a Bachelor of Science Degree

### *Graphic Design*

The graphic design major provides core courses in art plus a series in design, including design fundamentals, image and content, colour theory, computer graphics for the visual artist, multimedia graphic design and topography. This major introduces students to the graphic design studio environment, including tools, materials, terminology and business practices. Students learn the basics of client contact, fulfilling a client's needs through concept drawings and preparing camera-ready artwork. They also become familiar with marketing, accounting and production schedules. Field trips to design firms are an integral part of the programme. In addition, students take courses in computer literacy, where there is particular emphasis on the use of computer software programmes in both design and illustration.

Each student in the Graphic Design major develops an electronic portfolio that documents his or his educational experiences from the first year through graduation.

Graduates receive a Bachelor of Science Degree.

## Mainstream Western or International Styles

- International standard business attire—global in influence, just as business functions globally.
- Haute couture

*Regional Styles:*

- Clothing of Europe and Russia
- Clothing in the Americas
    - o United States mainstream fashion

For example: bland Sears catalogue fashion, regional styles such as preppy or Western wear.

o United States alternative fashion

These fashions are often associated with fans of various musical styles.

- Clothing in Asia
- Clothing in Africa
- Clothing in Oceania

## Fashion Design Jobs in India

The scope of fashion design jobs in India is unlimited for India is a land of many colours, which are reflected in the vibrant clothing of the Indian People. India has an ancient textile heritage that is celebrated in our great epics. One of the greatest feats of textile engineering is mentioned in the Mahabharata, when the evil Dushasan attempts to disrobe the Princess Draupadi. His efforts are in vain, for Lord Krishna helps Draupadi retain her honour by ensuring her sari is of an unending length. Thus, no matter how much fabric Dushasan tries to pull off, he finds that yet more fabric remains draped over Draupadi's body. Truly an amazing feat of fashion designing!

Fashion design may be a relatively new field in India, however the Indian people have always had a sense of fashion. From the traditional hand woven cotton and silk sarees of South India to the woollen Phirans of Kashmir, decorated with delicate floral embroidery and the colourful wraps of the tribal communities of

North Eastern India to mirror work and tie and dyed fabric in Rajasthan and Gujarat, fashion has many manifestations across the length and breadth of the country.

The scope for fashion design jobs in India is immense as Indians have increasingly become more conscious about their appearance and seek to enhance it in every way. Dressing well and fashionably has become the norm. Clothing companies need to hire people in a variety of jobs, ranging from Fashion designers, textile designers, models, retailers, buyers and merchandisers, to provide end-to-end solutions to their clients.

The scope of fashion design jobs is therefore vast and extends beyond India's markets to global markets too. Fashion designers such as Ritu Kumar, Raghavendra Rathore, Rohit Bal, J.J. Valaya and Ritu Beri are known worldwide. Institutions such as the National Institute of Fashion Technology (NIFT) provide training to budding fashion designers to develop their talent and become entrepreneurs in the fashion world. The India Fashion Week has become an international fashion event, with buyers from international stores making an appearance to transact business.

With more and more Indians dressing up and focused on looking good, there is an increasing awareness about fashion in India. The scope of fashion design jobs in India looks like it's cut out for success.

This page of Naukri hub concentrates on Fashion Design jobs in India. On this page, we endeavour to list the relevant Fashion Design job openings, employment search in Fashion Design as well as the Fashion Design job listings. Through these India job openings, you can get to know about the various employment opportunities prevalent in India. We have attempted to put on this page Fashion Design Jobs in India, Fashion Designing career, freelance Fashion Design jobs, Job Openings in India.

***Fibre 2 Fashion:*** Fibre-to-fashion job site provides unlimited information and opportunities exclusively for the Fashion Designing Professionals. In this profession there are jobs like Designer, Product Line Manager, Sales & Marketing Coordinator, Product Controller, Creative Director etc. Job seekers have a variety of export job options, import jobs, documentation jobs and well-qualified candidates to find entry level export-import jobs in the Fashion design industry.

***Textile and Fashion Jobs*:** The top job site of India displays the largest number of jobs in fashion designing.

***Fashion Design Recruitment:*** Fashion-Jobs, he number one source of fashion jobs and talent for the fashion, home, beauty, graphics and entertainment industries. The site has a track record of connecting the right people with the right fashion jobs has made us the most trusted recruiter in the world.

## Future Outlook

Do you want a career with constant challenge, unbelievable excitement, tremendous creativity and an ever-present shot at overnight stardom? You should add fashion to your list of potential careers. Few jobs can offer you comparable perks and rewards.

***Starting a Career in Fashion:*** Although fashion designers and runway models get the most press, there are many careers in the fashion world. Photographers, magazine reporters, seamstresses and A/V technicians, all help bring fashion exhibitions together. If any of the above occupations interests you, then read on.

***Hit the Books—Study the Basics:*** The more one studies, the farther one goes. This is as true for fashion as it is for any other occupation. By going to school and mastering the basics, you develop a deeper understand of your particular craft. In fashion design school, for example, you will learn the importance of colour coordination, material selection, character development and even tangential areas such as lighting and marketing. These studies will prove invaluable once you get started. Fashion is one of the most competitive industries out there. You can become a success overnight, but you can also remain in obscurity forever. If you study in a formal setting first, the odds of success go up exponentially. This is true regardless of what occupation you pursue in the fashion world. Photographers for fashion magazines are just as competitive as the designers themselves.

***Job outlook:*** People will always want to look good. This much was true before the MTV generation, but it is especially true now. Thus, fashion careers will flourish in the many years to come. Whether you work as a designer, model, or photographer, expect there to be plenty of work out there for you. Be prepared to travel however. In this particular industry, it's not uncommon to find yourself in random cities around the world. New York one minute; Tokyo the next.

*What does it mean to study Fashion?*

If you decide to study for a fashion career, you'll learn to design clothing and accessories or the fabrics and materials they're made of.

*What kind of person does well in Fashion careers?*

If you've watched Heidi Klum's reality show "Project Runway," you've had a glimpse of the many kinds of designers who pursue careers in fashion. No one personality has the edge in the creative, public, fast-paced, ever-changing world of style. You'll need to have a great eye for line and colour and you'll need to be able to convey your designs to you clients—verbally and visually. If you buy fashion magazines and keep up with trends, you've already been studying for your fashion career.

***Studies that Lead to a Fashion Career:*** Though self-taught designers exist and though a few designers have begun their careers as unschooled apprentices, your best route to a fashion career is a bachelor's degree from an accredited fashion design school. There, you'll learn sketching, computer-aided design and business skills. You'll develop your portfolio of examples of your unique designs for potential employers.

*Where do Fashion Studies Take you?*

You might get hired by a specialty or department store; you might design for the mass market; you might freelance or work for yourself. If your goal is to one day have your own line, be inspired by Tommy Hilfiger, who insists that "with some talent and great marketing, you can literally build a fashion empire." Most fashion designers earn from $35,000-$75,000 annually.

*What's it Like to have a Career in Fashion?*

The highest salaries go to designers with good business sense and the ability to deliver on deadline. Design can involve long hours and lots of travel, especially when preparing for shows. Still, if you've watched reality design shows, you know that nothing beats the thrill of seeing your designs on the runway.

## Job Description and Activities

Fashion designers work on the design of a clothing range. Some may focus completely on a specialist area, such as sportswear, children's wear or accessories.

The main markets they design for are haute couture, designer ready-to-wear and high street fashion. Developments in technology mean that a designer ready-to-wear product can be produced as a high street version in under six weeks.

Depending on level of responsibility and the company, a designer may work to their own brief or be given a brief to work towards (including specifications in relation to colour and fabric) and develop a product from this.

***Typical Work Activities:*** The main areas are:

- High street fashion, where the majority of designers work and where garments are manufactured in their thousands. Influences play a key role in this design process and the turnaround of 'young fashion' in particular can be quite rapid.
- Ready-to-wear. Many designers will also produce ready-to-wear collections, although these are produced in relatively small numbers.

- Haute couture. This requires large amounts of time working on the production of individual garments.

Tasks depend on the market the designer is producing for, but core responsibilities include:

- creating/visualising an idea and making a sketch by hand or using computer aided design (CAD);
- analysing trends in fabrics, colours and shapes;
- keeping up to date with emerging fashion trends;
- planning and developing ranges;
- working with others in the design team, such as buyers and forecasters, to develop a product to meet the brief;
- liaising closely with sales, buying and production teams to ensure the item complements other products;
- developing a pattern that is then cut and sewn into sample garments;
- sourcing, selecting and buying fabrics;
- adapting existing designs for mass production;
- supervising the making up of sample garments;
- overseeing production;
- negotiating with customers and suppliers;
- managing marketing, finances and other business activities if working on a self-employed basis.

Experienced designers with larger companies may focus more on the design aspect, with pattern cutters and machinists preparing sample garments. In smaller companies these and other tasks, may be part of the designer's role.

## Entry Requirements

Although this area of work is open to all graduates and Diplomates, a degree in the following subjects will increase your chances:

- fashion;
- textiles;
- knitwear;
- art and design;
- graphic design.

Diplomates face increased competition from graduates. Although sometimes possible, entry without a degree or HND is increasingly unlikely and you would need to be able to prove that you have already gained expertise and experience in the industry. Graduates and Diplomates from non-fashion/textile-related courses would also need to gain experience in the industry to demonstrate they have a real passion and aptitude for fashion design.

A pre-entry postgraduate qualification is not a requirement but an MA in Fashion/Textile Design can improve opportunities, particularly for designers from other academic areas. MA courses in specific areas of fashion requiring slightly different skills and experience can be helpful in gaining related employment. For example, children's wear not only requires an interest in this area but also knowledge of sizing and textile properties; menswear may require knowledge of pattern cutting and tailoring where appropriate.

Companies may be reluctant to consider candidates without previous experience in the industry. Work experience of any kind in a design studio is highly desirable. Experience in retail can also be useful. New graduates may be able to gain experience working with designers in Italy, France or America before starting in the UK.

Employers usually expect to see a portfolio that clearly demonstrates the ability to design. Potential candidates will also need to show evidence of the following:

- creative flair, including an eye for colour and a feel for fabrics;
- design and visualising skills, either by hand or through computer aided design (CAD);
- practical skills, including pattern cutting;
- a proactive approach;
- commercial awareness and business orientation;
- self-promotion and confidence;
- interpersonal, communication and networking skills;
- negotiation and influencing skills;

- team-working skills;
- organisational and time management skills.

Competition for design jobs is intense throughout the industry, particularly in women's wear design. Other areas, such as children's wear and menswear, are less competitive due to the smaller numbers of fashion students specialising in these areas. You may need to seek opportunities to work your way up from roles such as design room assistant or pattern cutter.

Top design houses rarely advertise their vacancies. Throughout the industry, employment opportunities are frequently secured via speculative applications and effective networking. It is, therefore, important to try to build relationships with more established designers and companies, regardless of whether you are seeking permanent or freelance openings. From 1 October 2006 it will be illegal to discriminate against candidates on age grounds but, in practice, age may continue to be used in selection criteria by some employers.

## Training

The training available to a fashion or clothing designer will not only depend on the courses taken prior to employment, but also on the company. Pre-entry fashion design courses aim to give students an idea of what to expect through practical teaching and placements. However, once in employment, specific development opportunities can be limited. The culture of the industry is very much that people learn while doing the job. Initially, training is likely to be restricted to learning about the practical processes used in an individual company.

During a designer's career, training opportunities are frequently limited in scope as career development may result in only subtle changes in work. However, larger firms may provide business and computer training, which could include computer aided design (CAD) or other specialist software, such as Photoshop and Illustrator, to help design patterns.

There are also various opportunities to undertake courses covering different or specialist aspects of fashion. These are offered as short courses or part-time degree/postgraduate options. Relevant course details are available through resources such as the Prospects Postgraduate Directory and Art and Design Postgraduate Courses.

## Career Development

As a trainee fashion clothing designer career development will depend on your specialism, experience and reputation. The type of company you work for will also influence the specific roles available and opportunities for career development. Progression can be slow, particularly at the start of your career. Being proactive and making contacts in the industry is essential in a sector where people frequently move jobs in order to progress their career and there is a lot of pressure to produce new ideas which are commercially viable.

Design room assistant is the most junior level role based in the design room. Typical responsibilities include making up sample cards, chasing fabric samples and pattern cutting, but also answering the telephone and making coffee. Assistant designer is a step up. In this role, there is the opportunity to have a creative input through proposing ideas for shapes, colours, moods and techniques, although you are unlikely to have much influence in major decisions. Other activities include making up mood and trend boards, drawing up technical specifications for manufacturers and some responsibilities for a small area of a range.

Designers make the decisions on colour and mood for the season and design the more important elements of the range. It could take up to five years' related experience to secure such a position. With several years' design experience, progression is available through senior designer roles to the position of head designer. At this level, you will have considerable responsibility regarding overall design decisions and influences for the range, but designers will do the actual design work.

Design and technical director positions represent further progression. Alternatively, designers may consider becoming self-employed or moving into related occupations, such as retail buying, photography, fashion styling or journalism.

## Modelling Career

A *modelling career* offers you myriad opportunities, travelling to exotic locales, getting pampered by beauty specialists, hobnobbing with celebrities and earning thousands of dollars a day. But modelling is not all about fun and glamour. A modelling agency helps a model with her portfolio, getting plum assignments and handles various aspects of her contract and clauses therein.

***What it takes to be a Model?:*** Women models are generally between 5'9 and 6'0 and weigh in the range of 120 -130 lbs. There are varied skin tones and face shapes that are doing the ramp these days so there is no definite facial prerequisites. The kind of look that is preferred tends to change every fashion season. From innocent to medieval to anorexic and classic beauty; the requirement is based on the needs of the client. Modelling is usually client driven.

The characteristics that go into making a successful model are partly practical and partly aesthetic. What is good for the print media is not suitable for the ramp. Though there are exceptions to this rule, most models fit a standard wardrobe. The other types of models are petite and larger size models. Juniors and children are also an essential part of the modelling industry. After all dimpled smiles and innocent gazes can sell millions worth of products.

Modelling is not just about looking good. You need to work on your facial expressions, posing, make-up, hairstyling and wardrobe. An aspiring model should be able to move her body gracefully. Dance and rhythmic gymnastics are good for conditioning as well as expression. Learning to portray facial expressions needs practice. Practicing in front of a full-length mirror can help you with this. Posing is also a critical element of modelling. A turn of the ankle, the movement of your hand and the tilt of your head—its the fine details that make the difference. You need to hone up your skills at becoming comfortable in front of the camera.

*Fashion models* are the supermodels whose faces stare out of Vogue, Harper's Bazaar and Elle. Runway models who walk the ramp for fashion houses like Versace, Gucci, Chanel and Calvin Klein among others, usually have long limbs and prominent facial characteristics.

As a model, you will have a professional hair stylist to weave magic with your hair. But as a professional model, you should be able to do your own hair. A versatile hairstyle, one that is not too short and neither too long. Understanding fashion can help a potential model in the making. When you are modelling for clothes, its advantageous to know how a particular fabric will drape or move. It is essential to have some knowledge about the fashion industry if you are planning on making a career out of modelling. Good teeth, well-groomed hands and feet, clear and glowing complexion and poise are the requisites of a successful model.

### *Modelling Avenues*

***Fashion Print Modelling:*** This involves modelling for display advertisements and print materials and is a well paying segment.

***Fashion Lingerie Modelling:*** Because of the nature of the product, the model has to have good body tone and proportions.

***Body Part Modelling:*** This is a special category that requires the model to display just a part of the body. Many a beautiful model may have hands and feet that look horrible. Hand models have long and slender and graceful hands and fingers. This is a niche-modelling segment.

***Commercial Modelling:*** Commercial models are used to sell soaps and shampoos, cars and insurance. These models look like ordinary moms, dads, students and teachers. Commercial models do not have any height, weight or size restrictions.

### *Modelling Agency*

A model can either decide to work on her own or work with an organization or modelling agency. An independent or freelance model needs to track down her assignments and follow up on the non-exclusive contracts and other requisites.

Fashion centres of Europe offer excellent campaign opportunities and growth prospects for modelling career. The American cities of New York, Los Angeles, Chicago and Miami are the American fashion modelling hubs. Commercial modelling agencies represent commercial models—models for clients, who are promoting items such as household goods, automobile, baby items and cosmetics. A fashion-modelling agency grooms its models for a glamorous career in fashion modelling.

### *Model Portfolio*

A model's portfolio is an important marketing tool especially in the initial stages of her career. This portfolio is an assortment of photos that showcase the model's personality and earlier assignments. The modelling portfolio needs to contain certain basics—a good head shot that brings forth your physical personality and charisma. There must also be some good full-length shots to show your body shape. A blend of photographs taken by different photographers would work well since variety could lend an interesting blend to your portfolio snaps. The model of today needs to also look at her web presence. A reliable model web site show-casing their models can help photographers and art directors in their search for new talent. The costs of listing on a modelling site can vary from initial free service to hundreds of dollars. Some models even have a web site of their own.

### *Lecturer in Fashion Design*

Creative Pattern Cutting

University College for the Creative Arts

The University College for the Creative Arts at Canterbury, Epsom, Farnham,

Maidstone and Rochester was formed on 1 August 2005 through the uniting

of two leading specialist art and design institutions: Kent Institute of Art & Design and The Surrey Institute of Art & Design, University College. With around 6,500 students, the University College offers strengths in education and research in art, design, architecture, media and communication.

We wish to appoint a motivated and inventive Designer with specialist skills in pattern cutting to support and enhance the reputation of one of the foremost Fashion courses in the UK. You will be able to supplement their technical skills with experience and understanding of other contextualising aspects of Fashion, such as its history and theory, styling, Illustration, manufacture and production and/or associated business and marketing.

You will typically have a good honours degree in Fashion or an appropriately related subject area. Experience of quality assurance, curriculum development and academic and administrative management on HE programmes, with a clear understanding of contemporary educational issues is a must. You will be able to contribute as an enthusiastic member of a dynamic team and be to inspire and motivate students. You will also be actively engaged with your relevant industries and demonstrate evidence of a significant commitment to relevant research interests.

## Fashion Merchandising

The Department of Fashion and Apparel Studies addresses the design, development, analysis, delivery and use of products and services. An industry-oriented approach is emphasized. Its programmes prepare students for dynamic careers in apparel design and fashion merchandising. All students gain skills in verbal, written and visual presentation, computer networking, product development, business communication and project management.

The Department offers industry-standard software in all majors. Extensive contracts and partnerships with business and industry enhance student opportunities and international linkages and winter session travel/study programmes enhance classroom instruction. Off-campus coursework is available through special arrangements with the Fashion Institute of Technology in New York City.

The Fashion Merchandising major studies the planning, production, promotion and distribution of products in fashion industries to meet consumer demand. Students learn to define and analyze target markets, design and use visual communication and plan and promote fashion products. Positions include fashion directors, merchandise buyers, corporate merchandise planners and marketing directors.

The Apparel Design major studies the conceptualization, design and pre-production of products for apparel-related industries. Students learn to translate inspiration into design, use technology to conceptualize and develop apparel design and prepare promotional presentations. Positions include apparel designer, design development coordinators and computer-aided design system managers.

Students interested in these business-oriented fields should contact the Department of Fashion and Apparel Studies, 211 Alison West, 831-8714.

2

# Career in Interior Designing

## Interior Designing

Interior design programmes prepare people to plan and design indoor spaces. Students learn drafting and graphic methods to express their designs. They learn to select furniture and furnishings to fit their space designs. They also learn about building codes and laws.

Where some people see a couple of walls where they might put up some artwork, you see a space to install bookcases and set up a corner home office. Where other people see a fading wingback chair, you can already see the chair's rebirth with new upholstery and restyled legs.

Does this sound like you? Are you imaginative, resourceful and open to new ideas? Do you consider yourself an artist who would love to use three-dimensional space as a canvas?

Yes, yes and yes? If so, interior design may be the programme for you. As an interior designer, you use problem-solving skills to take the needs and desires of a client and translate that information into plans and designs for a particular indoor space.

The types of indoor spaces you might work with span an exciting range. You might work with a residential space such as a living room or a kitchen. Or you might design a commercial space such as a gallery, an office building, or a movie cinema. You could design a children's waiting room in a hospital or a lounge area in an airport.

Interior designers do more than decorate walls, add ornamental lighting fixtures and upholster furniture. They combine aesthetic appeal with functional quality. In other words, they are concerned not only with how good a space looks, but also how well it functions as a space that people can use.

As a student in this programme, you learn the basics of how to communicate visual ideas about three-dimensional space onto paper. You learn to do this by both manual sketching and computer programmes.

You also study the historical and sociological developments in interior design so that you learn from the past. This also teaches you to restore past technologies such as Victorian furniture and help preserve them for future use.

You learn about using colour, textiles, drapery and different kinds of furniture. You also focus on your own studio time, developing what you've learned into your own design projects. These are just a few of things you learn and study in an interior design programme.

Many schools offer accredited interior design programmes where you can earn a diploma, or an associate, bachelor's, or master's degree. Both a diploma and associate degree typically take two years of full-time study after high school. A bachelor's degree usually takes four years and a master's degree from two to three years after that."

***College Preparation:*** You can prepare for this programme by taking courses in high school that prepare you for college. This typically includes four years of English, three years of math, three years of social studies and two years of science. Some colleges also require two years of a second language.

***Introduction to Business***

*General Computer Applications*

*Computer Graphics*

*Home Furnishing*

*Drafting, Architectural*

*CAD Design and Software*

*Blueprint Reading*

*Art History*

*Drawing and Painting*

*Computer-assisted Art*

*Art Portfolio*

*Marketing*

*Home Furnishings Production*

***Undergraduate Special:*** You must also submit a portfolio of recent and original work. Portfolio requirements and guidelines vary from programme to programme. However, typically, your portfolio should contain drawings from three-dimensional sources.

You may be able to apply to an undergraduate programme without a portfolio. Some schools allow you to apply to their college or university as an undecided major. Then, after completing certain prerequisite studio art courses, you can apply to enter the programme.

Most colleges also require good scores on one of the following:

- American College Testing (ACT) exam
- Scholastic Aptitude Test (SAT)

***Graduate Admissions:*** Admission to graduate programmes is competitive. You need a bachelor's degree, good grades and good test scores on the Graduate Record Exam (GRE) General. You also need to submit letters of recommendation and a statement of purpose

There are two kinds of master's degree programmes: ""first-professional"" and ""post-professional."" If a school offers a first-professional programme, your bachelor's degree does not have to be in interior design or even visual arts-related

If a school offers a post-professional programme, all applicants must already have a bachelor's degree in interior design. To such a school, you must submit a portfolio. It should contain the most polished design projects from your work as an undergraduate interior design student."

***Typical Course Work:*** This undergraduate programme typically includes courses in the following subjects:

- Art History

- AutoCAD (Computer-Aided Design) for Interior Design
- Building Systems
- Colour
- Computer Drafting Studio
- Contract Design Studio
- Drafting Studio
- Foundation Drawing
- Furniture Design Studio
- History of Furniture and Architecture
- Human Factors in Ambient Environment
- Interior Codes and Construction
- Interior Design Communications
- Interior Design Studio
- Interior Materials and Finishes
- Lighting
- Perspective and Rendering
- Residential Design Studio
- Three-Dimensional Design
- Two-Dimensional Design
- Workplace Design

Course work in master's degree programmes varies, depending on whether the programme is first- or post-professional. As a first-professional graduate student, you have to complete a set of foundational art courses similar to many of the courses listed above. In addition, you would take advanced courses that explore in greater depth certain fundamental topics in interior design. These topics might include lighting, human factors and marketing and contracts issues. As a post-professional graduate student, your work is usually very individualized, depending on your interests and preferences.

***Things to Know***

Getting a diploma or an associate degree in interior design typically prepares you to be only a design assistant and not a professional interior designer. However, it also provides a useful introduction to this programme of study. If you decide afterwards that this programme is truly right for you, you can apply to get a baccalaureate or graduate degree.

Many states require you to be licensed before you can practice. Even when licensing is not required, a potential employer or client wants assurance of your professional competence and educational background. Passing the certification exam given by the National Council for Interior Design shows these things about you; it also qualifies you for licensure where necessary.

### *Interior Designing*

Retail display assistants design and create displays for the windows and departments of retail outlets.

***Work Activities:*** Retail display assistants, also known as visual merchandisers or window dressers, design and create window and floor displays for retail outlets. Their displays are used to encourage and promote sales and make stores attractive places in which to shop. Typical projects might include dressing the window of a clothes shop or recreating a fully furnished room on the floor of a furniture shop or department. Retail display is more commonly being referred to as 'visual merchandising' (VM).

Most large retail chain stores have central design teams who plan and coordinate displays for all their company's shops. Having an image that customers can identify is very important. Most of their time is spent in a drawing office/studio, usually based at company headquarters. They produce plans, drawings, instructions and photographs of displays and send them to all the relevant outlets. Retail sales assistants use the instructions that they have been sent to recreate the display in their own store. Regional display managers are responsible for making sure that the stores in their region are following instructions carefully and putting together displays that are up to standard.

Displays need careful preparation. Display assistants begin by choosing an appropriate theme (usually a seasonal event, such as Christmas) and measuring the display area to be used. These measurements may be used to make scale drawings.

They then have to decide what the overall colour scheme is going to be, what props they need and how the display is to be arranged and lit. Display assistants may then have to make any props that cannot be hired or borrowed. Putting up displays can be hard work. Display areas are often cramped, confined spaces. Props and merchandise have to be lifted and moved very carefully as they may eventually be sold.

***Personal Qualities and Skills:*** As a retail display assistant, you need the following skills and qualities:

- Creativity and imagination.
- An ability to visualise your ideas both on paper and in three-dimensional form.
- Willingness to change some of your ideas to suit the house style or image of your employer or client.
- Self-motivation, initiative and an ability to work alone.
- Knowledge of typography and production techniques.
- Physical fitness and stamina (building a display can be hard physical work).
- An understanding of health and safety measures (working in confined spaces or with power tools can be dangerous).
- Business skills (if you are working on a freelance basis).

***Pay and Opportunities:*** Pay rates for retail display assistants vary. The pay rates given below are approximate. Retail display assistants earn in the range of £190—£240 a week, rising to £300—£370. Higher earners can make around £460 a week. Earnings for self-employed, freelance display assistants vary depending on the scale of the project they are working on. Retail display assistants usually work a basic 39-hour week. However, late finishes and weekend work may be required from time to time, especially as deadlines approach.

Employers include large retail chain stores and supermarkets; their central design teams may be based at the company HQ—often in London and the Southeast. Independent retailers are more likely to use freelance designers, who both design and assemble displays.

Entry to this work is competitive.

The following information is sourced from government statistics.

The government's definition of types of jobs is slightly different to that used in this programme. For this type of job, the most relevant government-defined occupation is 'Merchandisers and window dressers'.

In 2001 there were 1,700 people working as 'Merchandisers and window dressers' in Scotland. 8 in every 10,000 employees working in Scotland were employed as 'Merchandisers and window dressers'.

***Entry Routes and Training:*** Most people enter this work after having taken a full-time course at college, such as a National Certificate or Higher National Certificate/Higher National Diploma in Art and Design, or a Higher National Certificate/Higher National Diploma in Visual Merchandising and Display.

Applicants are required to submit a portfolio of work.

***Qualifications:*** Usual entry requirements for Art and Design courses are:

- some Standard Grades for National Certificate level
- a suitable National Certificate or 1/3 Highers for Higher National Certificate/Higher National Diploma level

However, entry requirements vary and alternative qualifications may be accepted—check prospectuses for details.

A portfolio of your art work will also be required.

***Adult Opportunities:*** Having a portfolio of relevant design work can be useful. However, in common with most jobs in design, entry is very competitive.

Entry requirements for relevant art and design courses at some colleges may be relaxed for applicants who have some relevant experience.

- 3% of retail display assistants are self-employed.
- 23% work part-time.
- 8% have flexible hours.
- 2% work on a temporary basis.

### *Interior Designers*

***Significant Points:*** Keen competition is expected for jobs in interior design because many talented individuals are attracted to careers as interior designers.

Individuals with little or no formal training in interior design, as well as those lacking creativity and perseverance, will find it very difficult to establish and maintain a career in this occupation.

About 3 out of 10 are self-employed.

Post-secondary education—especially a bachelor's degree—is recommended for entry-level positions in interior design; licensure is required in 23 States, the District of Columbia and Puerto Rico.

***Nature of the Work:*** *Interior designers* draw upon many disciplines to enhance the function, safety and aesthetics of interior spaces. Interior designers are concerned with how different colours, textures, furniture, lighting and space work together to meet the needs of a building's occupants. Designers are involved in planning the interior spaces of almost all buildings—offices, airport terminals, theaters, shopping malls, restaurants, hotels, schools, hospitals and private residences. Designers help to improve these spaces in order to boost office productivity, increase sales, attract a more affluent clientele, provide a more relaxing hospital stay, or increase the building's market value.

Traditionally, most interior designers focused on decorating: choosing a style and colour palette and then selecting appropriate furniture, floor and window coverings, artwork and lighting. However, an increasing number of designers are becoming more involved in designing architectural detailing, such as crown molding and built-in bookshelves, or planning layouts of buildings undergoing renovation, including helping to determine the location of windows, stairways, escalators and walkways.

Interior designers must be able to read blueprints, understand building and fire codes and know how to make the space accessible to the disabled. Designers frequently collaborate with architects, electricians and building contractors to ensure that their designs are safe and meet construction requirements.

Despite the varied building spaces interior designers work with, almost all projects follow the same design process. The first step in developing a new design is to determine the needs of the client, known as programming. The designer usually will meet face-to-face with the client in order to find out how the space will be used and to get an idea of the client's design preferences and budget.

For example, the designer might inquire about a family's cooking habits if the family is remodelling a kitchen or ask about a store or restaurant's target customer in order to pick an appropriate design. The designer also will visit the space and take inventory of the existing furniture and equipment as well as identify the any potential design problems and the positive attributes of the space.

Following the initial meeting with the client, the designer will formulate a design plan and estimate the costs on the basis of the client's goals and budget. Today, designs often are created with the use of computer-aided design (CAD), which provides a more detailed layout and also allows for easier corrections than sketches made by hand. Once the designer has completed the proposed design, he or she will present it to the client and make revisions on the basis of the client's input.

When a design concept has been finalized, the designer will begin specifying the materials, finishes and furnishings required, such as furniture, lighting, flooring, wall covering and artwork. In addition, depending on the complexity of the project, the designer will need to prepare drawings and submit them for architectural review and approval by a construction inspector to ensure that the design meets all applicable building codes.

If a project requires any structural work, the designer will need to work with an architect or engineer for that part of the project. Most designs also will require the hiring of contractors to do such technical work as lighting, plumbing, or electrical wiring. When necessary, the designer will choose qualified contractors and write up work contracts.

Finally, the designer will develop a timeline for the project and ensure that it is completed on time, including coordinating the work schedules of contractors if necessary. The designer will oversee the installation of the design elements and after the project is complete, the designer, together with the client, will pay follow-up visits to the building site to ensure that the client is satisfied with the final product. If the client is not satisfied, the designer will make all necessary corrections.

Designers who work as in-store designers for furniture or home and garden stores offer their design services in addition to selling the store's merchandise. In-store designers provide services similar to those offered by other interior designers, such as selecting a style and colour scheme that fits the client's needs or finding suitable accessories and lighting. However, in-store designers rarely visit their clients' spaces and are limited in using only a particular store's products.

Interior designers sometimes supervise assistants who carry out their creations and perform administrative tasks, such as reviewing catalogues and ordering samples. Designers who run their own businesses also may devote a considerable amount of time meeting with clients and contractors, developing new business contacts, examining equipment and space needs and attending to business matters.

Although most interior designers do many kinds of projects, some specialize in one area of interior design. Some specialize in the type of building space—usually residential or commercial—while others specialize in a certain design element or type of client, such as health care facilities. The most common specialties of this kind are lighting, kitchen and bath and closet designs. However, designers can specialize in almost any area of design, including acoustics and noise abatement, security, electronics and home theaters, home spas and indoor gardens.

Three areas of design that are becoming increasingly popular are ergonomic design elder design and environmental—or green—design. Ergonomic design involves designing work spaces and furniture that emphasize good posture and minimize muscle strain on the body. Elder design involves planning interior space to aid in the movement of the elderly and disabled, such as widening passageways to accommodate wheelchairs. Green design involves selecting furniture and carpets that are free of chemicals and hypoallergenic and selecting construction materials that are energy efficient or are made from renewable resources.

***Working Conditions:*** Working conditions and places of employment vary. Interior designers employed by large corporations or design firms generally work regular hours in well-lighted and comfortable settings. Designers in smaller design consulting firms or those who freelance generally work on a contract, or job, basis. They frequently adjust their workday to suit their clients' schedules and deadlines, meeting with the clients during evening or weekend hours when necessary. Consultants and self-employed designers tend to work longer hours and in smaller, more congested environments.

Interior designers may work under stress to meet deadlines, stay on budget and please clients. Self-employed designers also are under pressure to find new clients in order to maintain a steady income.

Designers may transact business in their own offices or studios or in clients' homes or offices. They also may travel to other locations, such as showrooms, design centres, clients' exhibit sites and manufacturing facilities. With the increased speed and sophistication of computers and advanced communications networks, designers may form international design teams, serve a geographically more dispersed clientele, research design alternatives by using information on the Internet and purchase supplies electronically, all with the aid of a computer in their workplace or studio.

***Training, Other Qualifications and Advancement:*** Post-secondary education—especially a bachelor's degree—is recommended for entry-level positions in interior design. In addition, 24 States, the District of Columbia and Puerto Rico register or license interior designers. Following formal training, graduates usually enter a 1-year to 3-year apprenticeship to gain experience before taking a national licensing exam or joining a professional association. Designers in States that do not require the exam may opt to take it as proof of their qualifications. The National Council administers the licensing exam for Interior Design Qualification (NCIDQ). To be eligible to take the exam, applicants must have at least 6 years of combined education and experience in interior design, of which at least 2 years constitute post-secondary education in design. Once candidates have passed the qualifying exam, they are granted the title of Certified, Registered, or Licensed Interior Designer, depending on the State. Continuing education is required in order to maintain one's licensure.

Training programmes are available from professional design schools or from colleges and universities and usually take 2 to 4 years to complete. Graduates of 2-year and 3-year programmes are awarded certificates or associate's degrees in interior design and normally qualify as assistants to interior designers upon graduation. Graduates with bachelor's degrees usually qualify for entry into a formal design apprenticeship programme. Basic coursework includes computer-aided design (CAD), drawing, perspective, spatial planning, colour and fabrics, furniture design, architecture, ergonomics, ethics and psychology.

The National Association of Schools of Art and Design accredits approximately 250 post-secondary institutions with programmes in art and design. Most of these schools award a degree in interior design. Applicants may be required to submit sketches and other examples of their artistic ability.

The Foundation for Interior Design Education Research also accredits interior design programmes that lead to a bachelor's degree. In 2005, there were 137 accredited bachelor's degree programmes in interior design in the United States, located primarily in schools of art, architecture and home economics.

After the completion of formal training, interior designers will enter a 1-year to 3-year apprenticeship to gain experience before taking a licensing exam. Most apprentices work in design or architecture firms under the strict supervision of an experienced designer. Apprentices also may choose to gain experience working as an in-store designer in furniture stores. The NCIDQ offers the Interior Design Experience Programme (IDEP), which helps entry-level interior designers gain valuable work experience by supervising work experience and offering mentoring services and workshops to new designers.

Following the apprenticeship, designers will take the national licensing exam or choose to become members of a professional association. Because registration or licensure is not mandatory in all States, membership in a professional association is an indication of an interior designer's qualifications and professional standing. The American Society of Interior Designers (ASID) is the largest professional association for interior designers in the United States. Interior designers can qualify for membership with at least a 2-year or higher degree and work experience.

In addition to national licensure and membership in a professional association, optional certifications in kitchen and bath design are available from the National Kitchen and Bath Association. The association offers three different levels of certification for kitchen and bath designers, each completed through training seminars that culminate in certification exams.

Employers increasingly prefer interior designers who are familiar with CAD software. Interior designers also increasingly need to know the basics of architecture and engineering in order to ensure that their designs meet building safety codes.

In addition to possessing technical knowledge, interior designers must be creative, imaginative and persistent and must be able to communicate their ideas in writing, visually and verbally. Because tastes in style can change quickly, designers need to be well read, open to new ideas and influences and quick to react to changing trends. Problem-solving skills and the ability to work independently and under pressure are important traits. People in this field need self-discipline to start projects on their own, to budget their time and to meet deadlines and production schedules. Good business sense and sales ability also are important, especially for those who freelance or run their own business.

Beginning interior designers receive on-the-job training and normally need 1 to 3 years of training before they can advance to higher level positions. Experienced designers in large firms may advance to chief designer, design department head, or some other supervisory position. Some experienced designers open their own firms or decide to specialize in one aspect of interior design. Other designers leave the occupation to become teachers in schools of design or in colleges and universities. Many faculty members continue to consult privately or operate small design studios to complement their classroom activities.

***Employment:*** Interior designers held about 65,000 jobs in 2004. Approximately 3 out of 10 were self-employed. About 2 out of 10 wage and salary interior designers worked in specialized design services. Another 1 out of 10 worked in architectural and landscape architectural services. The remaining of interior designers provided design services in furniture and home-furnishing stores, building material and supplies dealers and residential building construction companies. Many interior designers also performed freelance work in addition to holding a salaried job in interior design or another occupation.

***Job Outlook:*** Employment of interior designers is expected to grow about as fast as average for all occupations through 2014. Economic expansion, growing homeowner wealth and an increased interest in interior design will increase demand for designers. However, interior designers are expected to face keen competition for available positions because many talented individuals are attracted to this profession. Individuals with little or no formal training in interior design, as well as those lacking creativity and perseverance, will find it very difficult to establish and maintain a career in this occupation.

As the economy grows, more private businesses and consumers will request the services of interior designers. However, design services are considered a luxury expense and may be subject to fluctuations in the economy. For example, decreases in consumer and business income and spending caused by a slow economy can have a detrimental effect on employment of interior designers. Nevertheless, demand from the health care industry is expected to be especially high because of an anticipated increase in demand for facilities that will accommodate the aging population. Designers will be needed to make these facilities as comfortable and homelike as possible for patients. Demand from businesses in the hospitality industry—hotels, resorts and restaurants—also is expected to be high because of an expected increase in tourism.

Recent increases in homeowner wealth and the growing popularity of home improvement television programmes have increased demand for residential design services. Homeowners increasingly have been using the equity in their homes to finance new additions, remodel aging kitchens and bathrooms and update the general decor of the home. Many homeowners also have requested design help in adding year-round outdoor living spaces.

Growth in home improvement television programmes and discount furniture stores has spurred a trend in do-it-yourself design, which could hamper employment growth of designers. However, some clients will still hire designers for a few initial consultations, but then will purchase and install the design elements themselves.

Some interior designers are choosing to specialize in one design element in order to create a niche for themselves in an increasingly competitive market. The demand for kitchen and bath design is growing in response to the increasing demand for home remodelling. Designs utilizing the latest technology, such as home theaters, state-of-the-art conference facilities and security systems are expected to be especially popular. In addition, demand for home spas, indoor gardens and outdoor living spaces are expected to continue to increase.

Extensive knowledge of ergonomics and green design are expected to be in demand. Ergonomic design has gained in popularity with the growth in the elderly population and workplace safety requirements. The public's growing awareness of environmental quality and the growing number of individuals with allergies and asthma are expected to increase the demand for green design.

***Earnings:*** Median annual earnings for interior designers were \$40,670 in May 2004. The middle 50 percent earned between \$30,890 and \$53,790. The lowest 10 percent earned less than $23,440 and the highest 10 percent earned more than $71,220. Median annual earnings in the industries employing the largest numbers of interior designers in May 2004 were as follows:

| | |
|---|---|
| Architectural, engineering and related services | $44,740 |
| Specialized design services | 42,000 |
| Furniture stores | 37,750 |

Interior design salaries vary widely with the specialty, type of employer, number of years of experience and reputation of the individuals. Among salaried interior designers, those in large specialized design and architectural firms tend to earn higher and more stable salaries. Interior designers working in retail stores usually earn a commission, which can be irregular.

For residential design projects, self-employed interior designers and those working in smaller firms usually earn a per-hour consulting fee, plus a percentage of the total cost of furniture, lighting, artwork and other design elements. For commercial projects, they might charge a per-hour consulting fee, charge by the square footage, or charge a flat fee for the whole project. Also, designers who use specialty contractors usually earn a percentage of the contractor's earnings on the project in return for hiring the contractor. Self-employed designers must provide their own benefits.

### *Areas of Design Specialization*

Designers work in a wide range of settings, both commercial and residential. Surveys indicate that a majority of designers practice at least part of the time in both the residential and commercial areas, although they tend to favour one or the other.

Because commercial designers must be knowledgeable about their clients' business needs, most concentrate within design specialties, such as designing for the hospitality or health care industries. Some restrict themselves to particular sub-specialties, for example, designing restaurants or residential kitchens and baths. A few work in highly specialized fields, like designing interiors for airplanes or yachts, or doing historic conservation or restoration.

***Skills for Success:*** As members of a service profession, interior designers' fortunes depend on their ability to satisfy clients. Thus, they must possess three important skill sets-artistic and technical skills, interpersonal skills and management skills:

- Designers must know how to plan a space and how to render that plan visually, so that it can be conveyed to the client. They must also be knowledgeable about the materials and products that will be used to create and furnish the space and about how texture, colour, lighting and other factors combine and interact to give a space its "feel" or "look." In addition, they must understand the structural requirements of their plans, the health and safety issues, building codes and many other technical aspects.
- Designers must be comfortable meeting and dealing with many kinds of people. They must communicate clearly and effectively, as well as be attentive listeners. Because they often must work collaboratively with architects, contractors and other service providers, designers need to be both good team leaders and good team players. They must be willing to negotiate and mediate when necessary to resolve problems.
- Designers must have excellent time and project management skills, since they frequently work on more than one project at a time, under demanding deadlines, while looking for new projects or clients. They must be able to develop and execute business plans in order to protect and grow their practices. They need to know how to market themselves to clients, to create informative and persuasive proposals and presentations and to maintain good client relationships.

***Occupational Outlook:*** According to the U.S. Bureau of Labour Statistics Occupational Outlook Handbook, about three out of 10 interior designers are self-employed—four times the proportion for all professional and related occupations. About two out of 10 wage and salary interior designers work in specialized design services. Another one out of 10 worked in firms offering architectural and landscape architectural services. The remainder of interior designers provided design services in furniture and home furnishing stores, building material and supplies dealers and residential building construction companies. Many interior designers also performed freelance work in addition to holding a salaried job in design or in another occupation.

## Interior Designers: What Do They Really Do?

One part artist, one part business professional and one part circus ringmaster, an interior designer is more than just a pretty face with an eye for beauty. From sketching, designing and arranging beautiful spaces to shopping for furniture and household accessories, there's no shortage of excitement in an interior design career. A job in this field can provide opportunities to travel and work with a variety of people. However, no job can be all glamour. Interior designers must be able to manage people, budgets and client relationships – all while designing spaces that are attractive, functional and meet building and safety codes.

Interior designers must have organizational skills and business know-how, as well as great taste and artistic ability. It comes as little surprise, then, that getting an interior design degree is quickly becoming essential for those wishing to enter the interior design job market. A degree is also a licensure requirement in many states.

### *Skills Needed*

***School Spotlight:*** AIU offers highly marketable associate's, bachelor's and master's degree programmes in career paths that are technically- oriented and in demand. Attend an AIU campus with interior design programmes near you:

Perhaps the most obvious essential trait for interior designers is artistic ability. You will need to provide sketches of your proposed designs for a space. CAD training may also come in handy, since the design process often involves using computer programmes to create two and three-dimensional renderings. You will also choose colours, furniture and materials to complement the design, as well as suit your client's needs for function, durability and accessibility.

The ability to work well with others is also a must. As an interior designer, you will communicate with clients to assess what they want and need in a space and then present your ideas for meeting those goals in a compelling way. Your responsibilities also include coordinating with architects, electricians, plumbers and others to complete the job in a timely and cost-effective manner.

Since interior designers complete a wide range of tasks and work with many different people, organizational skills are important. You are responsible for keeping the project on budget and on schedule. You will need to document your process and the products used and manage contracts and negotiations on your client's behalf. In addition to these things, you need a basic knowledge of building and safety codes to ensure that your design meets all necessary requirements.

***What is An Interior Designer?:*** Interior designers are creative, imaginative and artistic. They also need to be disciplined, organized and skilled business people. Combining knowledge with aesthetic vision, interior designers work with clients and other design professionals to develop design solutions that are safe, functional, attractive and meet the needs of the people using the space.

As is the case with any career, the practice of interior design can be rewarding and fulfilling if hard work prevails. Excelling at interior design requires energy, technical proficiency, vision and dedication.

***Keys to Success:*** As members of a service profession, interior designers' fortunes depend on their ability to satisfy clients. Thus, they must understand artistic and technical requirements of a project, interpersonal communication and management strategies.

- *Artistic and Technical Requirements:* Interior designers must know how to plan a space and how to present that plan visually so that it can be communicated to the client. Interior designers must also know about the materials and products that will be used to create and furnish the space and how texture, colour, lighting and other factors combine and interact to make a space. In addition, interior designers must understand the structural requirements of their plans, the health and safety issues, building codes and many other technical aspects.

- *Interpersonal Communications:* Interior designers must be comfortable meeting and dealing with many kinds of people. They must communicate clearly and effectively, as well as be attentive listeners. Because they often must work with architects, contractors and other service providers, interior designers need to be both good team leaders and good team players. They must be willing to negotiate and mediate when necessary to solve problems.
- *Management Strategies:* Interior designers must have excellent time and project management abilities since they frequently work on more than one project at a time under demanding deadlines. Interior designers must understand business planning and they need to know how to sell their ideas to clients, create informative and persuasive proposals and presentations and maintain good client relationships.

## Interior Designer Jobs

Interior designer jobs and vacancies are available across the UK. As an Interior Designer you will plan and supervise the design and execution of interiors and their furnishings and to organise the various arts and crafts essential to their completion. A professional interior designer provides a full consultancy service on projects from design concept to completion. You must be imaginative with the ability to generate fresh solutions from a variety of briefs combined with excellent visual ability and the detail knowledge to implement your concepts. Excellent communication skills are essential are you will be client and consultant facing from inception to completion and possess an aptitude for working and contributing to a design team.

It is highly beneficial as an Interior Designer to have a good understanding of AutoCAD or Microstation and experience with Photoshop and Adobe CS could be an added bonus. You will be degree qualified or have professional qualifications.

### *Working Conditions*

The work environment is usually quite pleasant; however, much time is spent away from headquarters, meeting with clients, contractors, or shopping. Designers must drive in all types of weather and sometimes work in buildings under construction. They often carry heavy, bulky sample books and sometimes have to climb ladders. Designers should have a valid California driver's license and some employers require workers to have the use of a car.

Designers have to cope with administrative details and masses of paperwork such as specifications, estimates and purchase orders. They must be able to deal tactfully with clients and supervise craft workers. Work is often performed under the pressure of deadlines and budget limitations.

### *Employment Outlook*

The following information is from the California Projections of Employment published by the Labour Market Information Division.

| | |
|---|---|
| Estimated number of workers in 1993 | 3,220 |
| Estimated number of workers in 2005 | 3,790 |
| Projected Growth 1993-2005 | 18% |
| Estimated openings due to separations by 2005 | 640 |

(These figures do not include self-employment or openings due to turnover.)

Continuous use of design services in residences and commercial establishments has increased the demand for qualified interior designers. Many consider the employment of an Interior Designer a luxury expense, so job opportunities are more frequent in prosperous times. When the economy turns down, chances of employment decrease markedly. Competition is very keen in this occupation, as there are more applicants than available job openings. Consequently, employers are becoming more selective and prefer to hire experienced job seekers instead of the trained but inexperienced. Additional job opportunities will result from the need to replace workers who leave the labour market.

***Wages, Hours and Fringe Benefits***

Designers may be paid a salary, commission, or salary plus commission. The median wage for designers in California is $15.06. New designers usually start at a lower wage. Commissions may be included. Experienced designers may earn $60,000 a year or more. Independent and self-employed designers often earn more; their incomes vary with the type, size and complexity of projects and upon their reputations and acceptance in the community. A small number of nationally known designers earn as much as $100,000 to $250,000 or more a year. Work hours are irregular to accommodate clients and may often involve nights and weekends.

***Entrance Requirements and Training***

A successful Interior Designer must expect a long hard struggle. To succeed one must possess a combination of talent, personality and a healthy competitive sense. Years of experience and training are necessary in order to advance. A beginning Interior Designer must accept jobs that offer basic practical experience and put up with long hours and difficult clients. Good computer skills, particularly with regard to drawing software programmes, are becoming more and more desirable.

Satisfaction in this work is found through artistic expression and interpretation of client's tastes. Interior Designers derive a great deal of pleasure from working with beautiful things and from seeing the results of careful planning and creative ideas. Interior Designers must work hard and be patient in order to succeed.

Entry into the profession of interior design usually requires graduation from an accredited college, university or professional school of interior design. The course of study should include principles of design, history, art, free hand and mechanical drawing and basic architecture. Correspondence or home study courses are not considered a substitute for formal education. New designers should expect to continue their education on the job. It generally takes three to five years of practical experience to become fully qualified. Assignments in selling or shopping provide excellent on-the-job training. Part-time or summer employment in the furniture department of retail stores or large architectural firms provide good basic training for students and may lead to a permanent job.

Interior Designers are eligible for membership in the American Society of Interior Designers (ASID) or the Institute of Business Designers (IBD) if they meet the membership requirements which include professional training and experience and the passing of the National Council for Interior Design Qualification (NCIDQ) examination.

### *Advancement*

Promotion for Interior Designers usually consists of assignment to more complex jobs with larger budgets and salary increases. Very talented Interior Designers may advance to the head of a decorating or design department. They may become interior furnishings coordinators or be given other supervisory positions in department stores or larger decorating or design firms. Designers with additional experience and consulting expertise may go into business for themselves

### *Finding Job*

Interior Designers find jobs through their school and by direct application to employers, private employment agencies, or the California Employment Development Department Job Service. It is advisable to prepare a portfolio of work for presentation.

## Careers and Education in Interior Design

For those of you thinking about a career in the exciting world of interior design, there are many things to consider. What kind of degree programme should you consider? What kinds of certifications do you need and how do you prepare for them? What are the different job fields within interior design? And, oh yeah, how are you going to pay for your education?

We've tried to help you out here with a series of introductory articles:

- *Introduction:* Interior designers (not to be confused with interior decorators) develop the blueprints of a room. Learn more about this profession and what it takes to become an Interior Designer.
- *Interior Design Schools:* This article covers educational requirements for entry into the field of Interior Design, including the difficulties of getting accepted, choosing the best school for you and the kinds of classes to expect. The importance of acceditation is also discussed.
- *Interior Design Degrees:* Similar to law and medicine, interior design certifications and licenses have strict requirements. This article discusses the degrees and certifications needed for individuals pursuing a career in the field.
- *Financial Aid:* Finding an interior design programme is only the first part of the battle—now, you actually have to pay for it! Funding sources for your education as an Interior Designer are discussed here.
- *Careers:* You will find many niche possibilities to pursue within your Interior Design career (such as architectural design and furniture design) and this article presents some helpful tips on planning for, finding and landing the perfect Interior Design job.

### *Interior Design Career*

Interior designing is the art of developing interiors, which are aesthetically appealing, technically sophisticated and satisfying the needs of the customer. Interior designers need to be creative, imaginative and artistic. They also need to be disciplined, organized, skilled and scientifically inclined. Interior design falls within the broader category of design—the professional area of activity concerned with planning and developing a wide variety of objects and spaces. It includes the planning and design of spaces for commercial, industrial and institutional uses. This guide to an interior design career will throw light on the interior designer profession. Find out the qualifications that are needed and the gamut of activities that are involved.

Interior designers are certified professionals who work to design internal environments that are pleasant, comfortable and functional. Some designers exclusively handle big projects like hotels, airports, major office buildings or interiors of theme parks. Others help clients in decorating their private homes. Designers prepare plans and other specifications for interior construction, furnishings, colours and lighting.

This has to be done keeping in mind the client's tastes, budgets and other requirements. Nowadays many designers use computer-aided designing methods to plan their layouts, as they are more precise and add colour to their imaginations. At the end of the planning phase, they present their designs to the client for approval and make requested changes to their plan. 3-D presentations, scaled dimensional space plans and animated walk-throughs allow an interior designer to present design ideas more effectively to the clients.

It is also essential that the plans meet state laws, including building codes. So it is imperative that an interior designer keeps pace with the regulations and requirements of the state. The design plans need to conform to structural requirements, health and safety issues and building codes.

Skills for a successful interior decorator:

- To be able to plan a space and render it visually appealing
- To have in-depth understanding of the materials and products used to create and furnish the space.
- Interior designers need to work collaboratively with architects, contractors and other service providers. Designers need to be both good team leaders and team players.
- It is essential to possess excellent time and project management skills, since there are situations when they need to work on more than one project at a time, under demanding deadlines.

A career in interior design involves balancing aesthetic aspects with functional strengths. A bachelor's degree in interior designing is a basic qualification that most employers would seek in a candidate seeking a career in interior design. A candidate must maintain a portfolio of projects worked on. It is also preferable to gain membership to a professional body.

***Specialization:*** Today's niche architectural market needs highly skilled and specialized interior designers. Most interior designers specialize in a certain type of design area whereas some concentrate on a sub-specialty. The work of an interior designer can extend to areas such as energy conservation, historic restoration and planning barrier-free facilities for the aged and the physically challenged. This guide to careers in interior design highlights some of the segments:

- Residential designers: Involved in new home construction and renovations
- Entertainment designers: Create interiors for theaters, clubs, restaurants, concert halls, pubs, theme parks and other entertainment venues.
- Institutional designers: Focus on projects such as child-care, educational and religious institutions.
- Health care designers: Create environments for hospitals, clinics, examination rooms, surgical suites, mobile units and health care facilities.
- Office designers: Focus on the special needs of the work environment, such as ergonomic design, lighting and acoustical requirements as well as space planning.
- Retail designers: Involved in commercial spaces such as boutiques, department stores, showrooms and shopping malls.

***Career Prospects:*** After graduating with a Bachelor of Science in Design degree, aspiring interior designers can take positions with design consulting offices, corporate design departments and government design agencies, working on consumer and industrial products, building and equipment systems and public and corporate communication projects. They can also find employment in interior design firms, architectural firms, furniture dealerships and any commercial setting such as health care, retail, or institutional. Interior designers can also carry on their profession as freelancers. Freelance interior designers have more freedom in picking and choosing their projects and exercise greater control over their plans.

***Interior Design Career—Prospects:*** The job market for interior designers looks upbeat and positive, with the rising demand for professional design of private homes, offices, restaurants, retail businesses and retirement and nursing homes. However, interior designing has become a highly competitive field with many young, dynamic and talented designers.

But with the increasing number of interior designers graduating these days, it is necessary for them to keep themselves updated with the latest trends and innovations so as to maintain a competitive edge. Earnings for Interior designers can range from $22,000 to $40,000 a year. Some established designers working with big clients earn six figure salaries whereas some small-scale freelancers hardly earn enough to stay in business.

### *Interior Design Careers and Jobs*

Interior designer Barbara Schlattman had a customer who yielded a simple request: "I want a retreat." So Schlattman — a graduate of the University of Houston and an active member of the American Society of Interior Designers who has owned her own design business since 1975—went to work on the complex project designed from this simple request.

"My job is to make it beautiful, make it happy and make it function," Schlattman says. After consulting with construction contractors and the customer, she thought of an elaborate design for a part of the house that is perhaps the room with the most privacy: the bathroom. And so, work began on the bathroom that would eventually win a national award from *The Wall Street Journal*.

In-home luxuries creating spa-like private retreat surroundings in the master bath are a new specialty, but the interior designer field has many such specialties. Some focus on residential design like Schlattman, while others work in business/commercial design such as hospitals, university buildings and corporate offices. Others specialize even further, designing only specific rooms like bathrooms or bedrooms.

The interior spaces of structures—private homes, public buildings and business or institutional facilities—is enhanced in function, safety and quality by interior designers' work, in a definition by the Bureau of Labour Statistics. Interior designers likewise plan interiors of as part of the renovation or expansion of exiting structures, the BLS notes.

Responsibility over the building's foundation or construction is why 22 states and the District of Columbia register or license interior designers by requiring the passing of the National Council for Interior Design Qualification exam. Some states will not allow workers to practice interior design until the NCIDQ test is passed, while others simply disallow use of the title of interior designer until passing.

The interior design career's biggest fields as of the 2002 BLS report include varied disciplines: architectural, engineering and related services as well as specialized design services and furniture stores.

"That's the beauty of being in this profession — you can really zero in," says Rosalyn Cama, owner of New Haven, Conn.,-based Cama Inc.

"It's harder and harder to be a generalist and say you can do it all. You not only need to know the industry, but the industry you are working for," she adds.

The end goal of serving the clients remains the same in other interior design specialties, although they may not be showered with similar lavish requests.

In 1980, Anita Baltimore started a company with four workers called Interior Design Services, Inc., that concentrated on designing offices. Since then, the design firm has branched out to architecture, sales, furniture and accounting. The company, based in Nashville, Tenn., now has more than 100 employees.

"I've been a busy, busy woman," says Baltimore, a former national president of the American Society of Interior Designers.

She has devoted most of her time, even after the company expanded, to office buildings. She has seen the industry blossom from the days of the 1960s when the main debate revolved around whether to build offices with open or closed walls. The job has become more sophisticated.

Now, rooms are being designed with the belief that a room's environment can affect productivity. The design of a retail store can boost or reduce sales, as can the lighting on certain clothing items.

"I used to have to try to explain years ago what I could do for them — what affects my expertise and knowledge can have on their office," Baltimore says.

Cama, the interior design owner from Connecticut, has specialized in mainly health care buildings, especially children's hospitals. Her designs focus on creating a safe, family-friendly hospital room by emphasizing multiple light sources (windows, lights), a trendy, modern colour scheme ("hopefully the white walls are a misnomer, meaning we've moved from the 1970s," she says) and a window that provides a nice view.

But Cama pays special attention to one part of the room: the foot wall, or the wall the child will be staring at. Why? "You have to make sure the patients or families aren't looking at any clinical stuff on the wall," Cama says.

An interior designer for 29 years, Cama has remained contemporary in her thinking by attending continuing education sessions offered through ASID, an organization she previously served as national president. She attends three or conferences a year, some as an attendee, others as a teacher.

"It's a job of ongoing changes," Cama says. "The industry changes, technology changes, methodology changes. If you're not keeping up on it then you're missing out."

*Interior Designers by the BLS numbers (2002):*

- Roughly one-third of the estimated 60,000 interior designers in the United States is self-employed.
- Nearly four of every five interior designers are women
- Chicago and New York are home to the most U.S. interior design firms

- Job outlook for interior designers is "average" through 2012.
- Median annual earnings $39,180 in 2002; middle 50% earned between $29,070 and $53,060

For the home retreat project, Schlattman needed to know bathrooms. And more. By the time she was done, a flowing waterfall filled the middle of the 35 x 28 ft. bathroom retreat, decorated with goldfish and orchids.

To the bathroom with carpeted floors and flesh-colour painted walls, the customer wanted an open atrium. "But no, that would be too dirty," Schlattman told her, so to give energy to the room, a 20-feet long skylight was used instead.

"She wanted to feel like she was bringing the outdoors, indoors," Schlattman says

One wall hid a treadmill. Another wall looked too bland and needed something interesting, so Schlattman ordered the installation of a fireplace.

By the end, the bathroom was larger than the house's dining room. When asked how much the price tag for the lavish bathroom was, Schlattman says he leaves the costs for the contractors and the customer and worries instead about the lighting scheme, the carpets and the colours. "My job is to listen to what my clients want and to guide them so no mistakes are made and so it still functions for them."

***Interior Design:*** *Creative Instincts + Training = Rewarding Career.*

Choosing a career in interior design can be a rewarding decision with the right information and guidance. Interior designers are three-dimensional artists who have the ability to visualize and carry out ideas based on creative instincts and training. They are also business professionals who understand that in a service profession such as interior design, successful careers depend on the satisfaction of clients. It is important that interior designers not only be creative and artistic, but also highly organized and efficient.

The road to a career in interior design begins with education. According to the Foundation for Interior Design Education and

Research (FIDER) (the national accrediting agency for college and university interior design education programmes), a professional interior designer is expected to:

- Analyze client's needs, goals and life safety requirements
- Integrate findings with knowledge of interior design
- Formulate preliminary design concepts that are aesthetic, appropriate and functional and in accordance with codes and standards
- Develop and present final design recommendations through appropriate presentation media
- Prepare working drawings and specifications for non-load bearing interior construction including reflected ceiling plans, lighting, interior detailing, materials, finishes, space planning, furnishings, fixtures and equipment in compliance with universal accessibility guidelines and all applicable codes
- Collaborate with professional services of other licensed practitioners in the technical areas of mechanical, electrical and load-bearing design as required for regulatory approval
- Prepare and administer bids and contract documents as the client's agent
- Review and evaluate design solutions during implementation and upon completion.

Interior designing, often mistakenly referred to as "interior decorating," is inherently different from decorating. Interior decorating refers mainly to a concern for the aesthetics of interiors. A decorator selects and applies finishes such as wall covering, paint and tile, then selects and arranges furniture and accessories, through colour and style coordination, to create the look and feel of a space.

Interior designers are also concerned with the aesthetics of an interior, though a designer is initially concerned with issues relating to an interior's function and accessibility. An interior designer uses his/her knowledge of interior construction, building codes, construction and finish materials, equipment and furnishings to create specialized drawings and documents used by contractors to build the space created by the designer. Throughout this process, the designer continuously generates and revises solutions to problems arising from the function of the space or issues regarding the health, safety and welfare of the public.

Because interior designers are largely responsible for providing safe, healthy environments for the public that are functional as well as aesthetically pleasing, it is essential for the beginning designer to receive a quality education. Earning a degree in interior design is also important due to increasing licensing requirements. Currently there are over twenty states or jurisdictions that have requirements regarding the practice of interior design.

Some states have legislation in place which state that you cannot even call yourself an interior designer without meeting requirements such as receiving a degree from an accredited design programme, or in some cases, passing the interior design qualifying exam administered by the National Council for Interior Design Qualification (NCIDQ). Every state has different regulations regarding the practice of interior designers. The state of Georgia, for example, has a title act, which requires that a practicing interior designer be registered in the state and have at least a 4-year professional degree. The state of Florida, however, has a practice act, which requires interior designers to receive a 2-year degree plus 6 years of experience under a licensed designer to practice as an "interior designer."

Before selecting the institution where you will study, check to see if the institution(s) you are interested in has a FIDER accredited interior design programme. FIDER, as mentioned previously, is responsible for the accreditation of design programmes that meet the high standards of design education by providing students with knowledge required for entry into the practice and profession of interior design. Some states and potentially more in the future, will require FIDER accreditation as part of licensing or practice regulations. There are many opportunities for careers in interior design. Typically, interior designers working with a firm will either practice residential or commercial design. Residential design relates to family dwellings, town homes, condominiums, or apartments. Commercial design includes design for the interiors of corporate offices, hotels, restaurants, banks, or other public commercial spaces. Opportunities are also available for interior designers to work in furniture dealerships, as historic preservationists, or more specialized fields such as lighting or kitchen & bath design.

Interior design is among several occupations projected for continued growth throughout the coming years and competition for design jobs will pose new challenges for young designers; however, highly skilled creative professionals will be valued and sought after by employers.

If you are interested in interior design as a career, get involved and ask questions. There are numerous resources available for students. Professional organizations such as the American Society of Interior Designers (ASID) and the International Interior Design Association (IIDA) offer answers to frequently asked questions including salary ranges, job opportunities and education information. The more informed you are now, the greater your chance will be for future success.

***Read an excerpt from the Vault Career Guide to Interior Design***

The domain of interior design is a varied one. Designers are known by the type of project they typically work on, whether commercial or residential. Project budgets can range from the low thousands to well over a million dollars. Style also varies: modern, classical, retro, etc. California, Texas, Florida and New York have the highest concentration of interior designers. New York and Los Angeles are the main design hubs in the United States, but interior design is growing in other metropolitan areas, like Atlanta.

From more traditional designers such as Mariette Himes Gomez to Anna Nicole's Bobby Trendy, designers are fast becoming celebrities in their own right. But just as today's hottest starlet can easily become tomorrow's old news, designers are also susceptible to the public's whims. Staying on top requires determination and hard work. Being consistently published and making the "Top 100" list put out by so-called shelter magazines like Architectural Digest and House Beautiful are musts for any high-profile designer.

Magazines and television portray interior design as a glamorous career of unlimited creativity and fun. Shows like Trading Spaces and Queer Eye for the Straight Guy depict designers spending their days selecting fabrics and colours, choosing furniture and objects. Within a half hour, a space has been transformed from atrocious to magnificent and all we see the designer do is select a few objects and explain their scheme. No time is spent explaining the gritty details: picking exactly the right elements and ensuring they fit properly and are available in the right finishes, checking that they are in stock, dealing with delays from the manufacturer and questions from installers.

What really goes on behind the scenes? How is that beautiful house featured in Elle Decor or Metropolitan Home actually created? A great deal of unspectacular but essential work goes on to make a project a success. This book will provide valuable insight only an insider can reveal: the truth behind the glossy pages, a look at the clients, what skills and qualifications are necessary to succeed and whether the field is really for you.

***The Industry:*** As of November 2003, there were over 10,000 interior design firms in the U.S., employing nearly 50,000 people. Small companies, employing only one to four people, are the most prevalent, accounting for nearly 7,000 of these firms.

But the interior design industry is highly fragmented—only 0.4 percent of all interior design companies have over 100 employees. This smaller scale makes for an atypical business environment. Compared to other professions like computing, banking or engineering, there are no conglomerates like Microsoft to work for, so most designers end up at a small to medium-size firm with fewer than 50 employees. According to the U.S. Bureau of Labour Statistics, in 2002 approximately 40,670 interior designers were employed in various design related businesses. This number does not include self-employed designers; when those individuals are included, the total number increases to about 62,000. But other studies suggest numbers as high as 65,000 to 75,000, primarily because there is no nationally consistent definition of what qualifies someone to be an interior designer.

***Demographics:*** Interior design is female-dominated, with women accounting for approximately 60-80 percent of employed professionals. These numbers fluctuate depending on whether architectural firms are included in calculations, since they tend to employ more male designers. According to the American Society of Interior Designers (ASID), 55 percent of practicing designers in the United States are between the ages of 35 and 54, with about 20 percent of designers over the age of 55 and 25 percent under age 34.

The Bureau of Labour Statistics reports that "interior design, along with other design fields, is growing at a faster-than-average rate nationally, when compared with other occupations." From 1999 through 2002, the number of employed interior designers grew by 35 percent. Increased growth is expected to continue through the year 2010 due to demand for design services in the following specialties: office, health care and hospitality. As reported by Interior Design magazine, the Top 100 Interior Design Giants collected a total of almost $1.5 billion in fees in 2003. The highest earners were office and retail design, accounting for almost 30 percent and 13 percent respectively. Other design specialties were not as fortunate. Residential design declined almost 12 percent as did financial institutions, which decreased 22 percent.

### *Career Information for Architecture, Interior Design and Construction Management Students*

*What is Architecture?*

Architecture (in Greek arch = "first" and tecnh = "craftsmanship") is the imaginative blend of art and science used in the design of buildings. A wider definition would include within its scope the design of the total built environment, from the macrolevel of town planning, urban design and landscape architecture to the microlevel of furniture. Problem solving, decision-making, team leadership and creativity are key elements in making architecture and lead to the tremendous excitement that comes from seeing a design idea become a physical reality.

*What is an Architect?*

Architects design buildings and as part of that activity they create drawings, build scale models, write specifications, letters and other documents, supervise or manage architectural projects. They also may teach architecture, carry out research, or give advice to building owners.

Most architects do not actually carry out the construction of the buildings they design. That is usually done by construction contractors. However, some architects do construction in a design-build company. Others may normally build smaller projects such as houses.

Architects also may develop projects on their own, alone or in conjunction with financial advisors, real-estate developers or others.

Architects can do more than design buildings. Some serve as consultants on a broad range of clients' needs such as long-term business planning, relocation planning, interior design, human resources and space-use planning, facility maintenance programming and hundreds of other services.

The practice of architecture is enriched by the cultural and ethnic diversity of the men and women who join the profession.

*What other professionals work with architects?*

Other professionals work for architects on a building project such as structural engineers, civil engineers, electrical and mechanical engineers, landscape architects, cost experts, acoustical specialists, lighting designers, interior designers, artists, photographers, city planners, facility managers, regional planners, land developers, real-estate firms, sociologists, demographers and many more.

*How do architects become involved in projects?*

In many cases, architects respond to requests for proposals published by private or public clients. This is one way that clients let interested professionals know that a project is pending so that they can try to be selected to design it.

Sometimes architects are invited to present their qualifications. This is usually followed by interviews and a presentation of past work in their portfolio.

Some architects participate in design competitions and then are hired to do a project when a jury, a group of people assembled by the client to evaluate architects, likes their preliminary design for a building selects them.

Many people are motivated to become architects because they want to literally make a better world. This is also why some architects try to become a visible and helpful part of their community;it is an important part of their outlook on life. This kind of involvement can also help clients see an architect as an agent for positive change.

Architects even make "cold calls" on potential clients to seek work. They also may be the initiators of projects themselves, especially if they are also the developer and client.

*What makes the profession worth practicing?*

For some architects, the excitement of architectural work comes from the mix of intellectual stimulation, technical challenges, making things and "getting your boots muddy" at a construction site. For others, the ability to be one's own boss and to make a living doing what one loves to do provides "psychic income". Since architectural practice options cover such a broad range of possibilities, from teaching and writing to construction supervision and management, you can define your own niche in the profession and satisfy your particular emotional needs.

Whatever the reason, most architects do what they do because they love it. Architecture is one of those professions where you may find yourself amazed that you can actually get paid to do something that you enjoy so much. While there are often more routine tasks that architects also have to wade through ask an architect about "shop drawings", for example—the positives usually far outweigh the more difficult challenges.

Besides, anyone who watches TV or movies knows what Hollywood knows; architecture is an inherently glamorous, stylish activity that attracts an interesting, diverse and talented group of professionals. There are as many ways to define architecture as there are architects; the potential is always there to make the profession your own.

### *Interior Design Careers—Future Outlook*

Have you ever wondered why the rooms that performers usually wait in before going on stage are green? Have you ever wondered why hospitals are usually bright white on the inside? Why are kitchens often yellow? If you study interior design, you will know how to answer some of these questions. Every aspect of a room potentially influences our moods, productivity and personality. Those with a career in interior design understand this intuitively.

*What the studies show*

Studies show that different colours, lighting and material can have a profound effect on a person. That's why interior design is as much a science as it is an art. Careers in this field require a deep understanding of psychology as well as an extremely discerning and creative eye. The wrong combination of furniture, wallpaper and carpeting can cause a great deal of anxiety. You'll need to study up on the basics before pursuing a career as an interior designer.

***Licensing is also Required:*** If not for your own edification, you'll need to go back to school because it's required by law. Interior design careers require certification and licensing. After all, you sometimes make substantial alterations to existing structures. And some of your materials might be potentially hazardous if used correctly. Unless you already know the do's and do not's of lead-based paints, then you will definitely need some formal training.

***The Good News:*** The good news is that there are a lot of potential clients out there. Every school, hospital, apartment, house and business could use some of your skills at some time or another. And this trend will only continue in the years to come. Urban renewal, suburban sprawl and an increasing population basically guarantee that there will be plenty of business for qualified interior designers. Careers in this field are pretty secure.

## Interior Designing & Decoration

*Q1. What is career of Interior decorator?*

*A1.* This is very true of places that we visit. First impressions of rooms, which please our aesthetic senses, tend to stay with us for a long time, long after we've physically left the place. Some people have an inborn talent to bring out the best in whatever is available and arrange things around to make a place beautiful.

And others who appreciate this aspect of decorating a place to achieve a desired effect can go in for training and become experts in the field. In fact, the field of beautiful interiors has made so much progress today that there are now two distinct fields *viz.*, interior decoration and interior designing. As compared to interior decoration, interior designing is a more specialised field and a lot of training and hard work goes into the making of a successful interior designer.

An interior decorator advises, chooses and then assembles furniture, furnishings, colour schemes, artefacts, etc. to do up a place. While on the other hand, an interior designer would actually design exclusive and unique furniture, fittings and artefacts, keeping in mind a client's tastes, personality, lifestyle and his budget.

*Q2. Do you have it in you?*

*A2.* A natural aptitude for working with colours, an artistic leaning, dexterity with hands, creativity, imagination, being able to visualise one's thoughts and an ability to translate one's thoughts effectively, patience and above all the ability to get along with people are some of the qualities a person requires for entry into this field. As an interior designer or decorator will be required to create an atmosphere as per the client's tastes, it is essential that he or she is able to understand, visualise and create something that will fulfil the client's needs, be aesthetically pleasing and keep to a budget too. An interior designer/decorator should be good at communicating his or her ideas to others. Good communication skills will be needed very often during the course of work. A good working knowledge of architecture helps too.

*Q3. What do you need in order to become an interior decorator or interior designer?*

*A3.* Well, there are many institutes offering courses in this field. The minimum academic qualification required for admission to such courses is 10+2 or its equivalent. Many polytechnics and vocational colleges offer courses in interior designing and decoration. The duration of these courses ranges from two to four years, depending upon the type of course and the institute identified for the pursuit of study. The course of study covers subjects like Art & Basic Design, Furniture Design, Furnishings & Fittings, Design, Construction & Materials, History of Interior Design, Services, Professional Management-Estimating & Budgeting, Display, Computer Aided Designing. Other areas covered included lettering, properties of materials and paint technology, exhibition design etc.

*Q4. What is the procedure for admission?*

*A4.* For interior designing, professional training can begin immediately after successfully completing the plus two examinations. Admission is usually based on performance at an aptitude test conducted to evaluate one's sensibility, drawing skills, especially technical drawing, spatial apperception and so on. There is a centre in Ahmedabad that offers a five year professional programme in interior design for students who have cleared the plus two exam with science subjects. Here the requirement is sixty per cent at the tenth standard level and fifty at the plus two or equivalent level. The course content is a good mixture of arts and technical subjects. Students are trained to look for optimum use in various types of materials. Some companies have their own specialised courses in interior design. In collaboration with Jenson & Nicholson, Exteriors Interiors offers a one-year programme in interior design. This course is open to all graduates and pre-graduates in any discipline.

*Q5. What are the Job prospects?*

*A5.* With the demand to create more working space increasing and with more and more people realising the need and importance of professional designers, interior designing as a profession has come to be recognised in our country. Opportunities are aplenty in architects' firms or in consultancy companies. Private business is a very lucrative option. One, however, has to be up to date on what's new, what's in, what's got maximum utility, pricing, etc. and bring about a good blend depending upon the client's requirements, budget and tastes. One also needs to be extremely dedicated about keeping commitments. To be successful in private practice, one also needs to have a native business sense.

*Q6. What is the List of institutes offering this course?*

*A6.* List of Institutes is-

- School of Interior Design, Centre for Environmental Planning Technology, Kasturbhai Lalbhai Campus, Navrangpura, Ahmedabad.
- Exteriors Interiors, S-49, Kalkaji, New Delhi; 47/1C, Hazra Road, Calcutta.
- J. J. School of Arts, Mumbai.
- Nirmala Niketan, 49, New Marine Lines, Mumbai.
- Sophia College B. K. Somani Polytechnic, Bhulabhai Desai Road, Mumbai.
- SNDT Women's University, Mumbai.
- South Delhi Polytechnic for Women, Lajpat Nagar, New Delhi

***Major Requirements***

An Interior Design degree from OSU will prepare you in a number of areas:

- history of furniture and textiles
- aesthetic and functional components of space planning
- floor plans, furniture styles, fabric, colour and design
- technical interior sketching
- principles of pricing, buying and displaying merchandise
- government regulations affecting interior design decisions

To study interior design at OSU, you enrol in the Department of Design and Human Environment located in the College of Health and Human Sciences. Your faculty adviser provides you with academic advising and career counselling. You have the opportunity to work with equipment in the computer-assisted design and drafting (CADD) lab. In your junior or senior year, you will be able to do a field experience. For specific course requisites within the major, see the OSU General Catalogue.

***Job Opportunities:*** With an Interior design degree from OSU, graduates have become interior designers for architecture studios, interior design firms and retail stores focusing on interior design. Graduates have also, specialized in a particular aspect of design, such as kitchen design or space planning. Graduates have also pursued careers as furniture company representatives who show lines to retail buyers.

Growth in population and increase in personal incomes are expected to spur demand for residential and commercial interior designers.

***Field Experience:*** The Interior Design Field Experience is a cooperative programme among the Department of Design and Human Environment, firms engaged in interior design and qualified junior and senior students who are preparing for careers in interior design. It combines the study of principles of interior design with on-the-job design experience.

There are two phases to the programme. Prior to field experience participation students participate in DHE 400 "Field Experience Orientation". DHE 400 includes opportunities for students to "job shadow" professionals in the field as well as learn job search and interviewing strategies. This is followed by the "Field Experience" (DHE 410), employment off campus during Summer Term. Internship sites are determined by mutual agreement of a company, the university supervisor and the student.

A variety of tasks assigned by the company provides the student with training and management experience. Most students in Interiors choose to enrol in "Field Experience" (DHE 410) during their final year of study and they receive academic credit for working in their professional field. During the employment period, supervision is directed by personnel in the employing firm. Contact between the student and university supervisor is maintained by weekly written reports and assignments. Many of the internships are paid and many result in offers of permanent employment. Evaluation of student performance is done by the supervising personnel at the firm and by the university supervisor. DHE 410 "Field Experience" is graded on an A-F basis.

***Interior Design Students Fast-track Their Careers***

Students from the University of Central England in Birmingham have been commissioned to design the new Jaguar Daimler Heritage Museum in Coventry as a Live Project to form part of their MA Interior Design.

Using new, post-optimal techniques to generate a new museum experience for Jaguar, the MA students from UCE Birmingham Institute of Art and Design (BIAD) were tasked with designing the new exhibition space. They formed part of a larger project team which drew on the skills and talents of established companies from across the country, with Birmingham-based architects Associated Architects commissioned to design the exterior structure and London-based Imagination developing the general marketing concept.

On Friday 30 March the students took their concept and ideas to the Jaguar Daimler Heritage Trust (JDHT) and presented to various directors involved in the project. The presentation involved not only aiding the directors to visualise the exhibition space itself, but also the new museum experience developed by the students. This included the ability to pre-plan and organise a visit before arriving at the museum using online resources, the post-optimal demeanour by which exhibits and information are delivered and a further continuation of the experience once a user left the space.

Subsequent to the presentation the directors of the JDHT have now requested that the proposal is taken forward to the trustees, so that this can inform and push forward the discussion of the new museum development..

Additionally, the entire student team were very much complemented on the creativeness of their design and ability to visualise a totally new experience, along with their professionalism in delivering such a high-end design concept. It is aimed that the project will now be exhibited at Design City, to be held at the NEC in January 2008.

Dr. Paul Bailey, course director for MA Interior Design, is pleased that the talents of students have been recognised. He said: "To be chosen for such a high profile project while still studying is an amazing achievement for these students. For a company with a profile like Jaguar to commission students is recognition of the abilities that these students have and the standard of work that is being produced has been on the same level as the established companies."

The joint venture between UCE Birmingham and the JDHT has been a successful partnership for both parties. John Maries, Executive Director of the JDHT said: "Over the next two years, the JDHT has many exciting opportunities in front of it, to develop its Museum activities. As an educational charity the JDHT is delighted that we are able to join students from UCE Birmingham, who will be demonstrating their creativity in how we might display our cars and artefacts."

### *Careers in Interior Design*

Designers work in a wide range of settings, both commercial and residential. A majority of designers practice at least part of the time in both the residential and commercial areas. Most commercial designers concentrate within design specialties, such as designing for the hospitality or health care industries. Some specialize further by designing restaurants or residential kitchens and baths, interiors for airplanes or yachts, or historic conservation or restoration.

The professional interior designer:

- analyzes client's needs, goals and life safety requirements.
- integrates findings with knowledge of interior design.
- formulates preliminary design concepts that are aesthetic, appropriate, functional and in accordance with codes and standards.
- develops and presents final design recommendations through appropriate presentation media.

- prepares working drawings and specifications for interior detailing, fixtures and furnishings in compliance with accessibility guidelines and applicable codes.
- collaborates with professional services of other licensed practitioners in the technical areas of mechanical, electrical and load-bearing design as required for regulatory approval.
- prepares and administers bids and contract documents as the client's agent.
- reviews and evaluates design solutions during implementation and upon completion.

### *Room by Room: Interior Design Careers*

***Commercial Interior Design:*** Commercial interior design focuses on the planning and design of public buildings and businesses — everything from retail stores to restaurants and from museums to hospitals. Since this type of design encompasses such a wide array of building types, some designers concentrate on very particular areas, including: entertainment (theaters, concert venues, theme parks), government/institutional (federal buildings, courts, libraries), health care (hospitals, clinics, examination rooms), hospitality/restaurant (nightclubs, restaurants, hotels), offices (both public and private areas) and retail/store planning (boutiques, department stores, shopping malls).

***Residential Interior Design:*** Just as the name implies, residential interior design focuses on the planning and/or specifying of interior materials and products used in private residences. Residential interior designers must be aware of such issues as child safety, family traffic patterns, home wiring and cable needs, switching and security systems and space requirements for home theatre electronics and computer hardware and the different challenges facing the design of single-family and multi-unit dwellings.

***Space Planner:*** A space planner creatively diagrams how a particular interior space will be organized—typically by working with commercial clients to maximize space within offices, institutions or other large structures to ensure the space is used efficiently. Space planners typically work alongside interior designers or architectural firms.

***Exhibit Designer:*** Most large museums employ an Exhibit Designer whose job it is to translate curatorial and educational ideas into gallery installations. Not only must the Exhibit Designer have a highly refined understanding of art objects and how they interact with one another in terms of colour and scale, but he or she must also be aware of the principles of conservation and preservation of art works so that they may be installed with proper light and safety precautions.

The Exhibit Designer works closely with the preparator and his or her crew to fabricate special exhibition cabinets, cases, pedestals, or display tables and supervises the installation of the exhibition or permanent installation and designs proper lighting once art works are in place.

***Lighting Designer:*** A room's lighting should be aesthetically pleasing as well as functional. A good lighting designer will use combine intensities, direction and colour of light to create pleasing spaces.

The knowledge and expertise of a lighting designer includes an interior design background that can help size up your architectural needs; an up-to-date knowledge of electrical codes; word on the latest technical advancements in lighting and control systems; and experience with maintenance and energy issues.

***Kitchen and Bath Designer:*** It's been recently estimated that nearly 60% of all home construction spending goes towards renovations—and the kitchen and bathrooms are the spaces of homes most often renovated. As a result, there's great potential for interior designers specializing in kitchen and bath design.

These designers focus on construction and mechanical systems, basics of kitchen and bath design, materials and estimation, lighting, universal design and theme application and computer-aided-drafting specific for the kitchen and bathroom design industry. There is even a professional organization—the National Kitchen and Bath Association (NKBA)—for this specialized form of interior design.

*What is an Interior Designer?*

An Interior Designer is a trained professional who deals with the functional and aesthetic qualities of the "inside" of buildings and spaces. The Council states that "the professional Interior Designer is qualified by education, experience and examination to enhance the function and quality of interior spaces for the purpose of improving the quality of life, increasing productivity and protecting the health, safety and welfare of the public."

Some of the tasks that you can expect to do as a professional interior designer may include:

- Analysis of the clients needs, goals and life and safety requirements.
- Integration of findings with knowledge of interior design.
- Formulation of preliminary design concepts that are appropriate, both functionally and aesthetically.
- Development and presentation of final design recommendations using appropriate presentation media.
- Preparation of working drawings and specifications for non-load bearing interior construction, materials, finishes, space planning, furnishings, fixtures and equipment.
- Collaboration with professional services of other licensed practitioners in the technical areas of mechanical, electrical and load-bearing design as required for regulatory approval.
- Preparation and administration of bids and contract documents as the client's agent.
- Review and evaluation of design solutions during implementation and upon completion of a project.

***Work Environment:*** As an interior designer, your work environment would depend in part on the design specialty you choose. Usually there are more opportunities in larger metropolitan areas.

Your work environment would also depend on your area of specialty. You may be employed by an interior design or architectural firm, a retail store, or the design department of a corporation or institution. Or you may become self-employed and work out of your own studio. In any case, you probably would not spend all of your time at your own headquarters since designers are frequently on the go, meeting with clients, contractors and suppliers or supervising at construction sites.

## Professional Opportunities in the Field

Everywhere you go today, you see the influence of interior designers. The public demand for design services has grown rapidly, especially in the last decade. With that growth has come a wider range of specialties in the field. Interior design serves the expanding residential design market, the diverse needs of businesses and solves problems relative to the interior environment.

Following is a sampling of some of the work opportunities that exist for interior designers:

- Interior Designer in a large or small firm, commercial or residential.
- In-house designer or draftsperson in an architectural office.
- Space planning and corporate office design.
- Facilities management.
- Specialized design, such as for health care or environments for elders.
- Specialized design, such as for the retail or hospitality industries.
- Universal design and ADA compliance specialist.
- Design of "green" interior environments or specialist in healthy interiors.
- Designer showroom employee or manager.
- Design product or manufacturer's representative.
- Self-employed residential interior design.
- Model Home design.
- Kitchen and bath design.
- In-house designer for builder or contractor.
- Retail furniture store designer and salesperson.

- Real estate sales and interior design follow-up.
- Historic preservation.
- Redesign and renovation of houses for resale.
- Custom furniture design.
- Aircraft, boat and recreational vehicle interior design.
- Lighting Design

The quality of any professional programme is ultimately measured by the number of its graduates who are professionally successful. Graduates of the BCC Interior Design programme are in demand because of the school's reputation for excellence in design education. BCC Interior Design graduates have found employment either as interior designers or in related fields and many are successful entrepreneurs, or are working for prestigious and respected design firms. BCC grads also hold important leadership positions in professional organizations representing interior designers.

## Interior Design Education, Schools and Degrees

A career in interior design offers tremendous opportunities for those who wish to wield their creative flair for design. Not to be confused with interior decorators who specialize solely in beautifying an internal area, interior designers interior design school graduates are professionals licensed to design and develop interior spaces.

## Job Description and Responsibilities

Interior design school graduates are responsible for developing the layout of an interior space from a holistic perspective, melding elements like architecture and decor. By planning the spatial use of an interior and adorning it with appropriate furnishings and fittings, interior designers create functional stylized spaces. Interior design school graduates are expected to:

*Effectively communicate with clients to understand their interior design needs*

*Conceptualize and present creative solutions to develop functional and aesthetically-pleasing interior spaces*

*Create and develop plans that document the design concept*

*Render computerized images*

*Obtain resources such as labour and materials*

*Ensure the design plan meets environmental, health and safety guidelines, as well as building and construction codes*

*Ensure optimal space management and placement of furniture and fittings*

*Implement and maintain budgets for design projects*

Coordinate design tasks with other industry professionals such as architects, plumbers, electricians, etc.

In addition, interior design school graduates need to be extremely organized and have excellent project and time-management skills.

Ideally, they should be customer-oriented and flexible in adapting to the changing needs of their clients. Being a team-player is also essential as interior designers must work closely with other professionals who are needed in the development and completion of design projects. Interior design school graduates possess a keen eye for detail and have an appreciation for all things artistic and aesthetic.

## Career Options after Interior Design School

Graduates of interior design schools can work as junior designers, design assistants, intermediate designers, senior designers and project managers. The areas of focus include space planning, visual merchandizing, the design of furniture and fixtures and much more; the career opportunities are certainly vast.

Graduates of interior design schools may choose to focus on residential or commercial work, while some designers even specialize in industry-specific areas such as hospitality or retail. Those who wish to further specialize in certain design disciplines may be required to pass examinations which grant them practice certification.

## Interior Decorating & Design Training Programmes

Penn Foster Career School is accredited by the Middle States Commission on Secondary Schools for high school and vocational-technical programmes and by the Accrediting Commission of the Distance Education and Training Council (DETC). Penn Foster Career School is affiliated with DANTES, which qualifies U.S. military personnel for tuition reimbursement. Many Penn Foster programmes are approved for U.S. Armed Forces veterans training benefits.

Penn Foster Career School offers affordable, all-inclusive pricing—among the lowest of all career schools—and 0% interest financing and customized payment plans.

## Undergraduate Studies in Interior Design

Interior Design involves the diverse business of creating peoples' immediate physical environment. Interior designers plan and furnish the interiors of homes, public buildings and commercial establishments. They analyze clients' needs and requirements, lay out space, prepare working drawings and specify interior finishes and furniture.

They also specify appropriate heating, cooling and lighting plans, prepare budgets and construction contracts; and supervise the installation of the design project. The OSU Interior Design programme is endorsed by the National Kitchen and Bath Association; graduates may apply to sit for the Certified Kitchen Designer and/or Certified Bath Designer examinations.

### *Interior Design School*

***Interior Design Degree? Campus and Online Schools:*** Interior designers use their education, creativeness and experience to help plan the space and furnish the interiors of private homes, public buildings and business or institutional facilities, such as offices, restaurants, retail establishments, hospitals, hotels and theaters.

Starting out in Interior Design, the designer must have the education to meet the demands of the job. Here we have established some of the most qualified colleges offering online interior design degrees.

### *PCDI—Professional Career Development Institute*

***The Professional Interior Decorating Programme:*** If you've ever looked at a room and wanted to transform it into a much more beautiful space, our home study course in professional decorating is for you.

We'll help you develop your creativity, showing you how to use colour, texture, fabric, style, furnishings, accessories, lighting and paint in a way that reflects your own personal taste and the tastes of a variety of clients, too.

Key advantages of our school:

- No campus attendance, no commuting, no deadline pressure
- All exams are open-book/open notes
- Learn at your own pace; graduate in as little as six months after taking the hotel and restaurant management courses!
- Graduate with a nationally accredited diploma
- Enrol any time and enjoy affordable, interest-free tuition

In this comprehensive, nationally accredited course, you'll learn about colour, design and lighting; scale and size; balance and harmony; texture, pattern, line, form and space; the psychology of colour; cool, warm and neutral colours; creating colour schemes; hue and value; how light and texture effect colour; artificial and natural lighting; direct and indirect lighting; and more.

You'll learn how to work with different types and styles of curtains and draperies, upholstery and slipcovers, lampshades, rugs and carpets, wall and window treatments, ceilings, furniture styles and materials and floor plans, for every room in the house! You'll also learn about setting fees, developing client relationships, working with suppliers and other essentials that interior decorators must have to start their careers.

There are no educational prerequisites or experience requirements to enrol. Convenient, practical home study training from PCDI makes learning decorating easy and fun.

### *Penn Foster Career School*

***Interior Decorator Programme:*** Interior Decorators can turn a ho-hum interior into something special. With home training from Penn Foster Career School you can develop your natural talent into a successful career as an Interior Decorator. In Penn Foster's convenient Interior Decorating programme you'll learn how to:

- Determine your client's needs and evaluate budgets
- Use the elements and principles of design and colour
- Choose the best treatments for floors, walls and windows
- Start and operate your own business

Upon graduation, Penn Foster will also provide you with a paid Certified Interior Decorator (CID) membership for six months. Penn Foster's Nationally Accredited Interior Decorator programme will teach you the skills you need to have a successful career working with home-builders, retailers, corporate clients and hotels. You could even start your own Interior Decorating business.

***American Inter Continental University:*** Associates Degree in Interior Design Bachelor Degree of Fine Arts in Interior Design

The Interior Design School programme at American InterContinental University at Los Angeles is structured to give graduates all the skills necessary to step right into a successful career as a residential designer, commercial designer, consultant, design specialist and more. AIU Los Angeles' Bachelor's Degree programme is accredited by the Foundation for Interior Design Education (FIDER) and includes an internship offering positions with top interior design firms and professionals, as well as the opportunity for students to work on their own design projects and build their portfolio.

### *American InterContinental University*

Buckhead—Atlanta, Georgia

The American InterContinental University campus at Buckhead—Atlanta, Georgia, offers Associates and Bachelors degrees in Fashion Design, Interior Design, Fashion Marketing,

Media Production and Visual Communications. AIU Interior Design School students are often taught by industry practitioners and given the foundation necessary to make decisions all the way from the early stages of building construction through to accessories and finishing touches.

### *Associate Degree in Interior Design*

Brooks offers Associate Degree programmes in Graphic Design, Fashion Design, Interior Design, Fashion Merchandising, Animation and Multimedia. Graduates of the Interior Design School programme are qualified to assist clients with the selection and arrangement of interior furnishings, materials and space planning and to perform the basic skills necessary to implement a design including taking measurements, providing cost estimates, preparing drawings and business documents and consulting with fabricators, installers and other support specialists.

### *International Academy of Design and Technology*

The International Academy of Design and Technology at Chicago, Illinois, offers degrees in Advertising and Design, Computer Graphic Design, Interactive Media, Interior Design, Fashion Design and Multimedia Production and Design. IADT Chicago's Interior Design School programme leads to a Bachelor of Fine Arts degree and the ability and knowledge necessary to enhance the function and quality of interior spaces.

### *International Academy of Design and Technology*

Graduates of The International Academy of Design and Technology's Interior Design School become specialists in the relationship between people and spaces. They learn how the built environment, designed properly and inventively, can improve working conditions, social discourse and the general quality of people's lives.

The International Academy is one of Canada's leading interior design school. The college opened in the fall of 1983, it currently has a student population of about 1800.

### *International Academy of Design and Technology*

Residential designers are responsible for more than making the wall paper match the crown molding, they are responsible for creating a mood that is a reflection of the person who is to inhabit the space.

Residential design is just one of the many careers that interior design degree students prepare for at the International Academy of Design & Technology, Tampa. Here are a few more exciting careers to consider...commercial design, contract design, model home design, drafting, computer aided design, facilities management and consulting.

At Harrington, all of our programmes are based on a cooperative enterprise between students and faculty, encouraging full participation in projects, discussions and critiques. Each programme offers real-world experience in interior design that puts you in position to begin a successful career—and courses that develop your individual creativity.

- Bachelor of Fine Arts
- Associate of Applied Science in Interior Design
- Diploma in Kitchen and Bath Design certificate

## Bachelor of Science in Interior Design

***Cooperative Education:*** Through the cooperative education system, students gain salaried practical experience to complement their expanding academic understanding of the discipline. Bachelor of Science in Interior Design students integrate six quarters of work experience in their five-year curriculum in cities all over the country and overseas. Most are employed by interior design and/or architecture firms, but they also work in other design-related offices, public agencies and commercial companies.

***Career Opportunities:*** The term "interior design" is often confused with interior decoration. The latter generally deals with the selection of finishes and furnishings for existing spaces and is concerned with the application of surface treatments. UC graduates enter the practice of interior design, which addresses interior space volumes and spatial sequences, designing each space, including the planning of furnishings and specifying surfaces.

Interior designers may focus on specialized roles such as design, space programming, office administration, marketing and public relations, computer applications, or historic preservation. An Interior Design degree can also lead to a career as a facility programmer, computer software designer, facility manager, product sales representative, or university professor.

***Definition and Nature of the Work:*** Interior designers plan and design the interiors of buildings. They work for interior design firms, architectural firms, retail stores and the design departments of large industries or institutions. Some have their own businesses. Interior designers often specialize in homes, hospitals, hotels, or banks. Some specialize in restaurants, stage sets, or the interiors of ships or airplanes.

When they plan the interior of a new building or the structural remodelling of an old one, interior designers usually work with architects. The architects consult with the interior designers about traffic patterns and may ask them to plan the placement of stairways, windows and doors, as well as cabinets and other built-in units.

Interior designers examine material samples before presenting a detailed plan and sketch to a client. (Paul Barton/ Corbis.)

Whether they are involved in the planning of the structure of a building or merely in the decorating of one or more rooms, interior designers give advice on colour schemes, window treatments and hardware and lighting fixtures. They also suggest finishes for walls, ceilings, floors and cabinets. They choose accessories, such as plants or paintings, that will accent an interior.

Interior designers talk with their clients to establish how much work needs to be done. They also take into consideration the clients' habits, tastes and budget requirements when they create their designs. They draw up floor plans or sketches, which are done more and more with computer-aided design, or

CAD, than by hand. Interior designers present these plans and sketches to clients along with colour charts, fabric swatches, photographs and sometimes even original designs for furniture. They also submit an estimate of the total cost of the job. They may have to revise their plans several times before the client approves them.

Once the plans for designs are approved, the interior designers supervise the actual work of decorating. They order materials and contract for the services of workers. They may shop for those furnishings that will not be custom made. They make sure that draperies are hung properly and that the furniture is arranged conveniently.

Designers who work for department stores and office or home furnishings stores usually only consult with customers at the store and they are expected to help sell the store's merchandise. They also make suggestions to the store's buyers about the wants and needs of customers.

***Education and Training Requirements:*** To become an interior designer, several years of formal education after high school are needed. There are two-to three-year programmes in professional schools of interior design, or a person can study interior design in a four-year programme leading to a bachelor's degree at a college or university. Some students go on to get a master's degree or a doctoral degree.

A student must also go through an informal one-to three-year apprenticeship before becoming an interior designer. Trainees often act as receptionists, buyers, or clerks while they learn the practical side of the interior design business. Experienced designers assist and advise trainees in such tasks as matching patterns, arranging furniture, dealing with customers and computer-aided design. After completing their training and taking an exam, interior designers may become licensed and members of the American Society of Interior Designers.

***Advancement Possibilities and Employment Outlook:*** Advancement depends on talent and experience. Interior designers can become supervisors in a design studio or in a department of a large store, manufacturing firm, or design firm. Some interior designers advance by opening their own businesses. Others teach in schools of design or work for magazines that deal with home furnishings and interior design.

There will be an increase in the employment of interior designers through the year 2014. More businesses and individuals are using their services. However, beginning workers may find heavy competition for jobs. Some decide to focus on a niche market in order to be competitive, such as designing for the elderly or the environment-conscious, or focusing specifically on kitchens and baths. The best jobs will go to those with talent, education and experience.

***Working Conditions:*** Interior designers work in studios or stores that range from small boutiques to larger, more luxurious settings. They are often out consulting with customers, manufacturers and workers. Some must travel long distances and carry heavy portfolios and sample books. They may visit expensive homes, buildings under construction and drafty warehouses. Interior designers often work long and irregular hours. They are usually under pressure to meet deadlines.

Interior designers need tact, patience and flexibility in order to deal with all kinds of customers. They should have artistic and creative talent as well as good business sense and the ability to solve problems. In addition, they should have computer skills in order to present their designs electronically.

***Earnings and Benefits:*** Earnings of interior designers vary widely. According to the U.S. Bureau of Labour Statistics, the top 10 percent earn $71,220 or more per year, while the bottom 10 percent of interior designers receive less than $23,440 per year. The median annual salary is $40,670 per year

### *Bachelor of Science in Interior Design*

Do you imagine yourself designing living spaces, shopping spaces, or spaces for fun, leisure and entertainment? Would you like to design spaces for single family homes, apartment high rises, retirement villages, or commercial spaces such as retail stores, offices, restaurants, hotels and hospitals? Or would you like to design showrooms for the kitchen and bath industry or create intricate drawings using computer-aided design for hospitals, corporate headquarters, or historic building renovations for revitalized urban centres?

If you imagine yourself designing such spaces, a bachelor's degree in interior design can help you attain the dream.

***Understanding the Profession:*** If you are thinking about working toward a career in interior design, you'll want to be informed every step of the way. You will want to start by understanding what interior design is—and what it isn't. For example, interior design is not the same as interior decorating. They are different fields and require different educational preparation.

***Interior Design Programme at ECU:*** The mission of the ECU interior design programme is to prepare leaders for the field of interior design who will be creative problem-solvers with a strong sense of social responsibility. Through a broad general education in the arts and sciences students prepare a lifelong foundation for understanding design within the larger context of culture and society. A strong major in interior design which integrates aesthetics and creativity with technology and an interdisciplinary knowledge base in addressing the human condition prepares students for assuming diverse roles in professional practice.

Honing intuitive abilities, mastery of critical thinking and interpretation of knowledge underlie abilities of graduates to pursue specialty areas of design, adapt to rapid changes in the profession and pursue graduate level training. Cognates in art, design and business augment competencies achieved in the interior design curriculum.

The art and science of design, tempered with a business acumen that encompasses a global economy, the interjection of computer-aided drafting, model building and image processing and other leading-edge technologies in the workflow and knowledge of the ethics and procedures in the interior design profession are all a part of the foundation of the ECU interior design programme. This context is the basis on which students programme, develop and evaluate their designs for effective environments for residential settings, retail, office facilities, health facilities and hospitality.

### *Course Descriptions*

***Admission and Retention:*** To declare the interior design major, students must have a cumulative 2.5 grade point average and complete IDSN 1180, 1181, 1281 and 1500 with a C or better. At ECU, students complete freshman and sophomore preparatory courses in interior design followed by admission into professional-level (junior-senior) courses based on an acceptable level of proficiency in studio work as shown in the sophomore portfolio review, a minimum cumulative 2.5 grade point average and minimum grade of C in the following courses: IDSN 1180, 1181, 1281, 1500, 2040, 2800, 2850; and Art 1905.

During the second semester of the sophomore year, students submit portfolios which contain representative work from specific courses: IDSN 1181, 1281, 1500, 2800 and 2850. This work is evaluated by the interior design faculty, who recommend whether students are prepared to enter the professional level (junior-senior) interior design courses. Students who do not meet the level of proficiency needed for the professional level courses have the opportunity to re-submit a portfolio a maximum of two additional times. Admission to professional level courses is competitive and limited.

***Topics of Study:*** As a student preparing for a bachelor's degree in interior design, you will be studying these topics:

- Colour theory and application
- Drafting and space planning
- Product knowledge of furniture, textiles and equipment
- Historic period styles
- Adaptive reuse design
- Computer-aided design and drafting
- Lighting and building systems
- Barrier-free design
- Residential design projects
- Commercial design projects such as office, healthcare, restaurant, hotel and retail facilities

- Professional business procedures
- Portfolio development

***Internships:*** As you near the end of your interior design course work, you will complete an intensive internship experience working for an interior design related business where you will practice your professional skills and enhance your job placement opportunities. You and your internship adviser will mutually decide the best internship site for you based on your career goals and geographic preferences.

***Interior Design:*** A dynamic, stimulating, demanding profession which draws on creative and practical talents.

***Programme:*** Students in the interior design programme at Western Michigan University become involved in the artistic and pragmatic planning of interior spaces. In the process they learn to draw upon information from the fields of:

- fine arts
- human ecology
- architecture
- graphic design
- industrial design
- psychology
- sociology
- anthropology
- environmental science

***Career:*** A career in interior design is filled with creative challenges and constant learning opportunities. It involves a commitment to developing environments that support life, living and work in a positive way that not only contributes to the desired image, but also enhances performance and productivity.

***Opportunities:*** Interior design graduates will find many career opportunities including both residential and commercial design. Residential designers develop the interiors of single family detached homes, apartments and condominiums, usually working directly with the end user. Commercial designers devote their energies to the design of offices, financial institutions, retail, hospitality and entertainment establishments, recreational facilities, health care, public and government institutions and specialized areas such as set design for TV/ theatre/film, exhibitions and kiosks.

***Accreditation:*** The interior design programme at Western Michigan University is committed to graduating designers capable of creating artistic and responsive interior spaces. Studio and classroom activities, field trips, speakers and required field experience are important components in developing creative problem solvers who integrate research and explore alternative solutions in the pursuit of total spatial development. The programme is accredited by the Council for Interior Design Accreditation and participates with art and industrial design in the accreditation of art and design programmes at WMU by NASAD (National Association of Schools of Art and Design).

## Interior Design Degrees

Get the expertise you need in Interior Design. Obtain information to become an Interior Designer, department store display designer, or an exhibit and museum display designer. This page lists schools and colleges offering Interior Design programmes, Interior Design degrees and Interior Design certification. Online Interior Design programmes are available here also.

### *American InterContinental University Los Angeles*

American InterContinental University at Los Angeles equips you to be successful in the today's competitive workplace. AIU at Los Angeles offers degree programmes in Business, Design and Information Technology. With a student population representing 100 countries you can learn in a diverse global setting.

Your career in design can begin now. Centred in Southern California, Brooks College Long Beach is your ticket to endless opportunities in Design and Fashion. These validated degree programmes in fashion design, merchandising, graphic design, interior design, multimedia, network technology and animation blend strong academic curriculum with useful, hands-on experience. In just two years you can acquire your degree and take advantage of large-based job placement assistance.

Open the doors to a rewarding professional future. Westwood College of Technology's Anaheim, CA, campus offers bachelor's and associate's degree programmes oriented toward computer-based technologies. Day and night class offerings make scheduling easy. And on-campus support services such as financial aid, career planning and job placement help to meet students' educational and professional needs.

Open the doors to a rewarding professional future. Westwood College of Technology's Inland Empire, CA, campus offers bachelor's and associate's degree programmes oriented toward computer-based technologies, such as computer-aided design, software engineering, animation and interior design. Day and night class offerings make scheduling easy. And on-campus support services such as financial aid, career planning and job placement help to meet students' educational and professional needs.

### *Colorado Interior Design Degrees*

***Westwood College, Denver North:*** Open the doors to a rewarding professional future. Westwood College of Technology's Denver North campus is located just minutes north of downtown Denver and is the largest campus in the Westwood College system.

Students can choose from a number of bachelor's and associate's degree programmes oriented toward computer-based technologies, such as computer-aided design, software engineering, animation and interior design. Day and night class offerings make scheduling easy. And on-campus support services such as financial aid, career planning and job placement help to meet students' educational and professional needs.

***Westwood College, Denver South:*** Open the doors to a rewarding professional future. Westwood College of Technology's Denver South campus offers bachelor's and associate's degree programmes oriented toward business, computer and information technology and design. Day and night class offerings make scheduling easy. And on-campus support services such as financial aid, career planning and job placement help to meet students' educational and professional needs.

***Florida Interior Design Degrees***

***International Academy of Design & Technology Tampa:*** Secure your future at the International Academy of Design & Technology in Tampa, FL. Prepare yourself for the rigours of a design career in fashion, graphic, interior, or web design in as little as 18 months. Let the International Academy of Design & Technology's extensive degree offerings and comprehensive job placement assistance services put you on the right track for success.

***Georgia Interior Design Degrees***

***American InterContinental University Buckhead:*** Set your career in design and business in motion at the American InterContinental University Buckhead. If you see yourself developing a future in Fashion Design, Media Production or International Business, AIU Buckhead is designed to give you the skills you need to be successful with an associate's or bachelor's degree programme. Small classes allow students to work closely with our world-class faculty members who have academic and real-world field experience.

***Bauder College, Atlanta:*** Bauder College of Atlanta, GA offers career-oriented curriculums to students pursuing professions in areas such as Business, Design and Information Technology. Our extraordinary teaching programme provides graduates with the skills they need to be successful in the marketplace. Take advantage of our comprehensive job placement services and enjoy the flexibility of day, afternoon and evening classes.

***Illinois Interior Design Degrees***

***Harrington College of Design:*** Now is the time to start designing your future. Situated in the center of Chicago's "Loop", the Harrington College of Design has provided for more than 70 years excellent professional design education programmes. Interior Design programmes are available for a associate degrees, bachelor's degrees and certificates. Classes are offered at flexible hours and work with your busy schedule. Financial aid is offered to qualifying students.

***International Academy of Design & Technology Chicago:*** Secure your future at the International Academy of Design & Technology in Chicago. Prepare yourself for the rigours of a career in design, technology, or e-commerce in as little as 18 months. Let the International Academy of Design & Technology's extensive degree offerings and comprehensive job placement assistance services put you on the right track for success.

***Kentucky Interior Design Degrees***

***Sullivan University System:*** All the schools in the Sullivan University System focus their programmes on career-specific courses only, enabling you to get the education you need faster. Click to learn more about accelerate certificate and degree programmes in business, technology, medicine, design, culinary arts and law.

***Michigan Interior Design Degrees***

***International Academy of Design & Technology Detroit:*** Turn your talent into a career at the International Academy of Design & Technology in Detroit. Certificate programmes are offered in Fashion Design, Interior Design and Visual Communications. Learn from instructors who are highly respected in the design field and attend classes when it's most convenient for you: days, evenings, or weekends.

***Nevada Interior Design Degrees***

***International Academy of Design & Technology Las Vegas:*** Turn your talent into a rewarding career at the International Academy of Design and Technology in Las Vegas. IADT offers degrees in Fashion Design, Interior Design, Web Design and Computer Graphics Design. Choose from day, evening, or weekend classes. Career placement assistance is available as well as financial aid for qualified students.

***New Hampshire Interior Design Degrees***

***Hesser College:*** Hesser College has been developing students for career excellence for more than 100 years. It's necessary to never forget that in today's competitive work force businesses are in search of only highly qualified people for the job. Hesser College has the ability to make you the qualified one employer are looking for. Choose to attend one of the five New Hampshire campuses. Pick from more than 25 career-oriented degree fields and enjoy the flexibility of our day, evening and Saturday classes.

### *New Jersey Carolina Interior Design Degrees*

***Berkeley College:*** Berkeley College has helped students prepare for business careers of all types since 1931. Our Bachelor and Associate degrees offer traditional academic learning with professional training and hands-on experience that is sure to put you in high demand with employers. Over 96% of our graduates are employed in positions within their chosen fields. With five campus locations in and around the New York Metropolitan area along with the personal attention you receive from small class sizes, how can you go wrong? Come experience the Berkeley Advantages and let Berkeley College start working for you!

### *New York Interior Design Degrees*

***Berkeley College:*** Berkeley College has helped students prepare for business careers of all types since 1931. Our Bachelor and Associate degrees offer traditional academic learning with professional training and hands-on experience that is sure to put you in high demand with employers. Over 96% of our graduates are employed in positions within their chosen fields. With five campus locations in and around the New York Metropolitan area along with the personal attention you receive from small class sizes, how can you go wrong? Come experience the Berkeley Advantages and let Berkeley College start working for you!

### *Canada Interior Design Degrees*

***International Academy of Design & Technology Toronto:*** Secure your future at the International Academy of Design & Technology in Toronto, Ontario. Prepare yourself for the rigours of a career in advertising design, computer graphics and animation, fashion design, fashion marketing, interior design, or digital film and television production in as little as 18 months. Let the International Academy of Design & Technology's extensive degree offerings and comprehensive job placement assistance services put you on the right track for success.

## Online Interior Design Degrees

***The Art Institute Online:*** Acquire the skills you need to enhance your career goals at The Art Institute Online. If you are a beginner or a seasoned professional, you can enhance your career opportunities with an associate's or bachelor's degree from The Art Institute Online. Degree programmes are offered in Multimedia & Web Design, Game Art & Design, Graphic Design and Digital Design. The Art Institute Online is a division of The Art Institute of Pittsburgh.

## Overseas Interior Design Degrees

***American InterContinental University London:*** Live in London and earn two degrees at once. American InterContinental University in London equips students with the knowledge, ability and conventional work experience you need to be successful in the world. At AIU London you are able to earn an American and British bachelor's degree in Business, Visual Communications, Interior Design, Fashion or Media Production. With students from over 100 countries in a central London location you can learn in a diverse global setting.

### *BA (Hons.) Interior Design*

Interior Design has never been so popular. Interior spaces are where people spend the greatest proportion of their time. Interior Design is a rewarding profession allowing the designer the opportunity to enhance people's everyday lives by creating new environments in which they work, live and play.

The BA(Hons.) Interior Design course at UCLan provides an interdisciplinary programme of study and is concerned with the interaction of design and technology through the creative process and imaginative use of materials. Offering more than just cosmetic solutions, interior design is a broad based professional discipline. The course encourages students to consider the challenges interior designers face in a range of engaging dynamic areas which include retail, the workplace, leisure, entertainment and life styles of the future. The course has a lively atmosphere where creativity is nurtured and students and staff enjoy an excellent working relationship. Interaction between students from other design courses is strongly supported through the use of common projects, social events and educational visits. Interior Design students are a crucial part of a broader community of designers who share a common drive and a commitment to delivering the best in design and creativity.

"Our first year was great as we got a broad grounding of design. We looked at different aspects of design such as architecture, building construction and developed drawing techniques as well as creative interior design skills. We get great feedback from projects and presentations that I find really supportive and helpful. After starting my second year I feel one step closer to commencing a career in design."

***Hannah Halford, Year Two Student:*** "At the beginning of the course we all went on a study tour to Barcelona that really helped break down barriers. It was a new experience that we all shared and enjoyed which helped us work together as a course team."

***Charlotte Hill, Student:*** Students wishing to take a year out of the full-time study programme have the opportunity to do so by intercalating. Students wishing to do so would be encouraged to do this at the end of Year 2, returning to complete their Year 3 study after a year working within industry. A place on the course will be reserved for that student for the 12 months they are away at work. Arrangements for this route would be self-directed by the students themselves.

## Career Opportunities

Many of the design skills that you will acquire and develop are transferable and can lead you into a variety of employment fields. Career opportunities include working as an Interior Design consultant, in-house designer for a specialist retail shop-fitting contractor, Computer 3D visualizer and corporate style consultant. In these jobs your role could take on many guises including consultancy business design partner or creative design team leader. Your role may even provide diverse opportunities to work in film, TV or theatre designing everything from performance sets to overall style adviser.

Alternative career directions can lead to teaching both in secondary and tertiary education. Successful students may also wish to continue their studies on one of the broad ranging MA programmes to further enhance their knowledge and skills base, exploring new and innovative areas of design.

### *Architects, Except Landscape and Naval*

- About 1 in 4 architects was self-employed—more than three times the proportion for all professional and related occupations.
- Licensing requirements include a professional degree in architecture, 3 years of practical work training and passing all divisions of the Architect Registration Examination.
- Architecture graduates may face competition, especially for jobs in the most prestigious firms; opportunities will be best for those with experience working for a firm while still in school and for those with knowledge of computer-aided design and drafting technology.

***Nature of the Work:*** People need places in which to live, work, play, learn, worship, meet, govern, shop and eat. These places may be private or public; indoors or outdoors; or rooms, buildings, or complexes and together, they make up neighbourhoods, towns, suburbs and cities. *Architects*—licensed professionals trained in the art and science of building design—transform these needs into concepts and then develop the concepts into images and plans of buildings that can be constructed by others.

Architects design the overall aesthetic and look of buildings and other structures, but the design of a building involves far more than its appearance. Buildings also must be functional, safe and economical and must suit the needs of the people who use them. Architects consider all these factors when they design buildings and other structures.

Architects provide professional services to individuals and organizations planning a construction project. They may be involved in all phases of development, from the initial discussion with the client through the entire construction process. Their duties require specific skills—designing, engineering, managing, supervising and communicating with clients and builders. Architects spend a great deal of time explaining their ideas to clients, construction contractors and others. Successful architects must be able to communicate their unique vision persuasively.

The architect and client discuss the objectives, requirements and budget of a project. In some cases, architects provide various predesign services—conducting feasibility and environmental impact studies, selecting a site, or specifying the requirements the design must meet. For example, they may determine space requirements by researching the numbers and types of potential users of a building. The architect then prepares drawings and a report presenting ideas for the client to review.

After discussing and agreeing on the initial proposal, architects develop final construction plans that show the building's appearance and details for its construction. Accompanying these plans are drawings of the structural system; air-conditioning, heating and ventilating systems; electrical systems; communications systems; plumbing; and, possibly, site and landscape plans.

The plans also specify the building materials and, in some cases, the interior furnishings. In developing designs, architects follow building codes, zoning laws, fire regulations and other ordinances, such as those requiring easy access by disabled persons. Throughout the planning stage, they make necessary changes. Computer-aided design and drafting (CADD) technology has replaced traditional paper and pencil as the most common method for creating design and construction drawings. Continual revision of plans on the basis of client needs and budget constraints is often necessary.

Architects may also assist clients in obtaining construction bids, selecting contractors and negotiating construction contracts. As construction proceeds, they may visit building sites to make sure that contractors follow the design, adhere to the schedule, use the specified materials and meet work quality standards. The job is not complete until all construction is finished, required tests are conducted and construction costs are paid. Sometimes, architects also provide post-construction services, such as facilities management. They advise on energy efficiency measures, evaluate how well the building design adapts to the needs of occupants and make necessary improvements.

Architects design a wide variety of buildings, such as office and apartment buildings, schools, churches, factories, hospitals, houses and airport terminals. They also design complexes such as urban centres, college campuses, industrial parks and entire communities. In addition, they may advise on the selection of building sites, prepare cost analysis and land-use studies and do long-range planning for land development.

Architects sometimes specialize in one phase of work. Some specialize in the design of one type of building—for example, hospitals, schools, or housing. Others focus on planning and predesign services or construction management and do minimal design work. They often work with engineers, urban planners, interior designers, landscape architects and other professionals. In fact, architects spend a great deal of their time coordinating information from and the work of, others engaged in the same project. Many architects—particularly at larger firms—use the Internet and e-mail to update designs and communicate changes efficiently. Architects also use the Internet to research product specifications and government regulations.

***Working Conditions:*** Architects usually work in a comfortable environment. Most of their time is spent in offices consulting with clients, developing reports and drawings and working with other architects and engineers. However, they often visit construction sites to review the progress of projects. Although most architects work approximately 40 hours per week, they often have to work nights and weekends to meet deadlines.

***Training, Other Qualifications and Advancement:*** All States and the District of Columbia require individuals to be licensed (registered) before they may call themselves architects and contract to provide architectural services. During this time between graduation and becoming licensed, architecture school graduates generally work in the field under supervision of a licensed architect who takes legal responsibility for all work. Licensing requirements include a professional degree in architecture, a period of practical training or internship and a passing score on all divisions of the Architect Registration Examination (ARE).

In most States, the professional degree in architecture must be from one of the 113 schools of architecture that have degree programmes accredited by the National Architectural Accrediting Board (NAAB). However, State architectural registration boards set their own standards, so graduation from a non-NAAB-accredited programme may meet the educational requirement for licensing in a few States. Three types of professional degrees in architecture are available through colleges and universities.

The majority of all architectural degrees are from 5-year Bachelor of Architecture programmes, intended for students entering university-level studies from high school or with no previous architectural training. In addition, a number of schools offer a 2-year Master of Architecture programme for students with a preprofessional undergraduate degree in architecture or a related area, or a 3- or 4-year Master of Architecture programme for students with a degree in another discipline.

The choice of degree depends upon each individual's preference and educational background. Prospective architecture students should consider the available options before committing to a programme.

For example, although the 5-year Bachelor of Architecture programme offers the fastest route to the professional degree, courses are specialized and if the student does not complete the programme, transferring to a programme offered by another discipline may be difficult. A typical programme includes courses in architectural history and theory, building design, structures, technology, construction methods, professional practice, math, physical sciences and liberal arts. Central to most architectural programmes is the design studio, where students put into practice the skills and concepts learned in the classroom. During the final semester of many programmes, students devote their studio time to creating an architectural project from beginning to end, culminating in a three-dimensional model of their design.

Many schools of architecture also offer post-professional degrees for those who already have a bachelor's or master's degree in architecture or other areas. Although graduate education beyond the professional degree is not required for practicing architects, it may be for research, teaching and certain specialties.

Architects must be able to communicate their ideas visually to their clients. Artistic and drawing ability is helpful, but not essential, to such communication. More important are a visual orientation and the ability to conceptualize and understand spatial relationships. Good communication skills, the ability to work independently or as part of a team and creativity are important qualities for anyone interested in becoming an architect. Computer literacy also is required for writing specifications, for two- and three-dimensional drafting and for financial management. Knowledge of CADD is essential and has become a critical tool for architects. Most schools now teach students CADD programmes and methods that adhere to the National CAD Standards.

All State architectural registration boards require architecture graduates to complete a training period—usually 3 years—before they may sit for the ARE, the third and final requirement for becoming licensed. Every State, with the exception of Arizona, has adopted the training standards established by the Intern Development Programme, a branch of the American Institute of Architects and the National Council of Architectural Registration Boards (NCARB).

These standards stipulate broad and diversified training under the supervision of a licensed architect over a 3-year period. Most new graduates complete their training period by working as interns at architectural firms. Some States allow a portion of the training to occur in the offices of related professionals, such as engineers or general contractors.

Architecture students who complete internships in architectural firms while still in school can count some of that time toward the required 3-year training period.

Interns in architectural firms may assist in the design of one part of a project, help prepare architectural documents or drawings, build models, or prepare construction drawings on CADD. Interns also may research building codes and materials or write specifications for building materials, installation criteria, the quality of finishes and other, related details.

After completing their on-the-job training period, interns are eligible to sit for the ARE. The examination tests a candidate's knowledge, skills and ability to provide the various services required in the design and construction of buildings. The test is broken down into 9 divisions consisting of either multiple choice or graphical questions; States give candidates an eligibility period for completion of all divisions of the exam that varies by State. Candidates who pass the ARE and meet all standards established by their State Board become licensed to practice in that State.

Most States require some form of continuing education to maintain a license and many others are expected to adopt mandatory continuing education. Requirements vary by State, but usually involve the completion of a certain number of credits annually or biennially through workshops, formal university classes, conferences, self-study courses, or other sources.

A growing number of architects voluntarily seek certification by the NCARB, which can facilitate an individual's becoming licensed to practice in additional States. This practice is known as "reciprocity." Certification is awarded after independent verification of the candidate's educational transcripts, employment record and professional references. Certification is the primary requirement for reciprocity of licensing among State Boards that are NCARB members. In 2004, approximately one-third of all licensed architects had NCARB certification.

After becoming licensed and gaining experience, architects take on increasingly responsible duties, eventually managing entire projects. In large firms, architects may advance to supervisory or managerial positions. Some architects become partners in established firms, while others set up their own practices. Graduates with degrees in architecture also enter related fields, such as graphic, interior, or industrial design; urban planning; real estate development; civil engineering; and construction management.

***Employment:*** Architects held about 129,000 jobs in 2004. Approximately 3 out of 5 jobs were in the architectural, engineering and related services industry—mostly in architectural firms with fewer than five workers. A small number worked for residential and nonresidential building construction firms and for government agencies responsible for housing, community planning, or construction of government buildings, such as the U.S. Departments of Defense and Interior and the General Services Administration. About 1 in 4 architects was self-employed.

***Job Outlook:*** Employment of architects is expected to grow about as fast the average for all occupations through 2014. Besides employment growth, additional job openings will arise from the need to replace the many architects who are nearing retirement and others who transfer to other occupations or stop working for other reasons. Internship opportunities for new architectural students are expected to be good over the next decade, but more students are graduating with architectural degrees and some competition for entry-level jobs can be anticipated. Competition will be especially keen for jobs at the most prestigious architectural firms as prospective architects try to build their reputation. Prospective architects who have had internships while in school will have an advantage in obtaining intern positions after graduation.

Employment of architects is strongly tied to the activity of the construction industry. Strong growth is expected to come from nonresidential construction as demand for commercial space increases. Residential construction, buoyed by low interest rates, is also expected to grow as more and more people become homeowners. If interest rates rise significantly, this sector may see a fall-off in home building.

Current demographic trends also support an increase in demand for architects. As the population of Sunbelt States continues to grow, the people living there will need new places to live and work. As the population continues to live longer and baby-boomers begin to retire there will be a need for more healthcare facilities, nursing homes and retirement communities. In education, buildings at all levels are getting older and class sizes are getting larger. This will require many school districts and universities to build new facilities and renovate existing ones.

Some types of construction are sensitive to cyclical changes in the economy. Architects seeking design projects for office and retail construction will face especially strong competition for jobs or clients during recessions and layoffs may ensue in less successful firms. Those involved in the design of institutional buildings, such as schools, hospitals, nursing homes and correctional facilities, will be less affected by fluctuations in the economy. Residential construction makes up a small portion of work for architects, so major changes in the housing market would not be as significant as fluctuations in the nonresidential market.

Despite good overall job opportunities some architects may not fare as well as others. The profession is geographically sensitive and some parts of the Nation may have fewer new building projects than others. Also, many firms specialize in specific buildings, such as hospitals or office towers and demand for these buildings may vary by region. Architects may find it increasingly necessary to gain reciprocity in order to compete for the best jobs and projects in other States.

In recent years, some architecture firms have outsourced to architecture firms overseas the drafting of construction documents for large-scale commercial and residential projects. This trend is expected to continue and may have a negative impact on employment growth for lower level architects and interns who would normally gain experience by producing these drawings. However, most firms will keep design services in-house and opportunities will be best for those architects that are able to distinguish themselves from others with their creativity.

***Earnings:*** Median annual earnings of wage and salary architects were $60,300 in May 2004. The middle 50 percent earned between $46,690 and $79,230. The lowest 10 percent earned less than $38,060 and the highest 10 percent earned more than $99,800. Those just starting their internships can expect to earn considerably less.

Earnings of partners in established architectural firms may fluctuate because of changing business conditions. Some architects may have difficulty establishing their own practices and may go through a period when their expenses are greater than their income, requiring substantial financial resources.

### *Drafters*

***Significant Points:*** The type and quality of post-secondary drafting programmes vary considerably; prospective students should be careful in selecting a programme.

Employment is projected to grow more slowly than average.

Opportunities should be best for individuals with at least 2 years of post-secondary training in drafting and considerable skill and experience using computer-aided design and drafting (CADD) systems.

Demand for drafters varies by specialty and depends on the needs of local industry, particularly architectural and engineering services and manufacturing.

***Nature of the Work:*** Drafters prepare technical drawings and plans used by production and construction workers to build everything from manufactured products such as toys, toasters, industrial machinery and spacecraft to structures such as houses, office buildings and oil and gas pipelines. Drafters' drawings provide visual guidelines; show the technical details of the products and structures; and specify dimensions, materials and procedures.

Drafters fill in technical details using drawings, rough sketches, specifications, codes and calculations previously made by engineers, surveyors, architects, or scientists. For example, drafters use their knowledge of standardized building techniques to draw in the details of a structure. Some use their knowledge of engineering and manufacturing theory and standards to draw the parts of a machine to determine design elements, such as the numbers and kinds of fasteners needed to assemble the machine. Drafters use technical handbooks, tables, calculators and computers to complete their work.

Traditionally, drafters sat at drawing boards and used pencils, pens, compasses, protractors, triangles and other drafting devices to prepare a drawing manually. Most drafters now use CADD systems to prepare drawings. Consequently, some drafters may be referred to as *CADD operators*. CADD systems employ computers to create and store drawings electronically that can then be viewed, printed, or programmed directly into automated manufacturing systems.

These systems also permit drafters to quickly prepare variations of a design. Although drafters use CADD extensively, it is only a tool. Persons who produce technical drawings with CADD still function as drafters and need the knowledge of traditional drafters, in addition to CADD skills. Despite the nearly universal use of CADD systems, manual drafting and sketching still are used in certain applications.

Drafting work has many specialties and titles may denote a particular discipline of design or drafting.

*Aeronautical drafters* prepare engineering drawings detailing plans and specifications used in the manufacture of aircraft, missiles and related parts.

*Architectural drafters* draw architectural and structural features of buildings and other structures. These workers may specialize in a type of structure, such as residential or commercial, or in a kind of material used, such as reinforced concrete, masonry, steel, or timber.

*Civil drafters* prepare drawings and topographical and relief maps used in major construction or civil engineering projects, such as highways, bridges, pipelines, flood control projects and water and sewage systems.

*Electrical drafters* prepare wiring and layout diagrams used by workers who erect, install and repair electrical equipment and wiring in communication centres, powerplants, electrical distribution systems and buildings.

*Electronics drafters* draw wiring diagrams, circuit board assembly diagrams, schematics and layout drawings used in the manufacture, installation and repair of electronic devices and components.

*Mechanical drafters* prepare drawings showing the detail and assembly of a wide variety of machinery and mechanical devices, indicating dimensions, fastening methods and other requirements.

*Process piping* or *pipeline drafters* prepare drawings used in the layout, construction and operation of oil and gas fields, refineries, chemical plants and process piping systems.

***Working Conditions:*** Most drafters work a standard 40-hour week; only a small number work part time. Drafters usually work in comfortable offices furnished to accommodate their tasks. They may sit at adjustable drawing boards or drafting tables when doing manual drawings, although most drafters work at computer terminals much of the time. Because they spend long periods in front of computer terminals doing detailed work, drafters may be susceptible to eyestrain, back discomfort and hand and wrist problems.

***Training, Other Qualifications and Advancement:*** Employers prefer applicants who have completed post-secondary school training in drafting, training that is offered by technical institutes, community colleges and some 4-year colleges and universities.

Employers are most interested in applicants with well-developed drafting and mechanical drawing skills; knowledge of drafting standards, mathematics, science and engineering technology; and a solid background in CADD techniques. In addition, communication and problem-solving skills are important.

Training and coursework differ somewhat within the drafting specialties. The initial training for each specialty is similar. All incorporate math and communication skills, for example, but coursework relating to the specialty varies. In an electronics drafting programme, for example, students learn how to depict electronic components and circuits in drawings.

Many types of publicly and privately operated schools provide some form of training in drafting. Because the kind and quality of programmes vary considerably, prospective students should be careful in selecting a programme. They should contact prospective employers regarding their preferences and ask schools to provide information about the kinds of jobs that are obtained by the school's graduates, the types and conditions of the instructional facilities and equipment and the faculty's qualifications.

Technical institutes offer intensive technical training, but less general education than do junior and community colleges. Certificates or diplomas based on the completion of a certain number of course hours may be awarded. Many technical institutes offer 2-year associate degree programmes, which are similar to, or part of, the programmes offered by community colleges or State university systems. Their programmes vary considerably in both length and type of courses offered. Some area vocational-technical schools are post-secondary public institutions that serve local students and emphasize the type of training preferred by local employers. Many offer introductory drafting instruction. Most require a high school diploma or its equivalent for admission. Other technical institutes are run by private, often for-profit, organizations sometimes called proprietary schools.

Community colleges offer curricula similar to those in technical institutes but include more courses on theory and liberal arts. Often, there is little or no difference between technical institute and community college programmes. However, courses taken at community colleges are more likely than those given at technical institutes to be accepted for credit at 4-year colleges. After completing a 2-year associate degree programme, graduates may obtain jobs as drafters or continue their education in a related field at 4-year colleges. Most 4-year colleges usually do not offer training in drafting, but college courses in engineering, architecture and mathematics are useful for obtaining a job as a drafter.

Technical training obtained in the Armed Forces also can be applied in civilian drafting jobs. Some additional training may be necessary, depending on the technical area or military specialty.

The American Design Drafting Association (ADDA) has established a certification programme for drafters. Although employers usually do not require drafters to be certified, certification demonstrates an understanding of nationally recognized practices and standards of knowledge. Individuals who wish to become certified must pass the Drafter Certification Test, which is administered periodically at ADDA-authorized sites. Applicants are tested on their knowledge and understanding of basic drafting concepts, such as geometric construction, working drawings and architectural terms and standards.

Individuals planning careers in drafting should take courses in mathematics, science, computer technology, design and computer graphics, as well as any high school drafting courses available. Mechanical ability and visual aptitude are important. Prospective drafters should be able to draw well and perform detailed work accurately and neatly. Artistic ability is helpful in some specialized fields, as is knowledge of manufacturing and construction methods.

In addition, prospective drafters should have good interpersonal skills because they work closely with engineers, surveyors, architects and other professionals and, sometimes, with customers.

Entry-level or junior drafters usually do routine work under close supervision. After gaining experience, they may become intermediate drafters and progress to more difficult work with less supervision. At the intermediate level, they may need to exercise more judgment and perform calculations when preparing and modifying drawings. Drafters may eventually advance to senior drafter, designer, or supervisor. Many employers pay for continuing education and, with appropriate college degrees, drafters may go on to become engineering technicians, engineers, or architects.

***Employment:*** Drafters held about 254,000 jobs in 2004. Architectural and civil drafters held 43 percent of all jobs for drafters, mechanical drafters held about 32 percent of all jobs and about 15 percent of jobs were held by electrical and electronics drafters.

About 44 percent of all jobs for drafters were in architectural, engineering and related services firms that design construction projects or do other engineering work on a contract basis for other industries.

Another 27 percent of jobs were in manufacturing industries such as machinery manufacturing, including metalworking and other general machinery; fabricated metal products manufacturing, including architectural and structural metals; computer and electronic products manufacturing, including navigational, measuring, electromedical and control instruments; and transportation equipment manufacturing, including aerospace products and parts manufacturing, as well as ship and boat building. Most of the rest were employed in construction, government, wholesale trade, utilities and employment services. Approximately 6 percent were self-employed in 2004.

***Job Outlook:*** Employment of drafters is expected to grow more slowly than the average for all occupations through 2014. Industrial growth and increasingly complex design problems associated with new products and manufacturing processes will increase the demand for drafting services. Further, drafters are beginning to break out of the traditional drafting role and do work traditionally performed by engineers and architects, thus also increasing demand for drafters.

However, drafters tend to be concentrated in slowly growing or declining manufacturing industries. CADD systems that are more powerful and easier to use also should limit demand for lesser skilled drafters as simple tasks are increasingly done quickly and easily by other drafters or other technical professionals, resulting in slower-than-average overall employment growth. Because some drafting work can be done in other locations using the Internet to send CADD files internationally, the offshoring of some drafting jobs also should dampen growth. Most job openings are expected to arise from the need to replace drafters who transfer to other occupations, leave the labour force, or retire.

Opportunities should be best for individuals with at least 2 years of post-secondary training in a drafting programme that provides strong technical skills, as well as considerable experience with CADD systems. CADD has increased the complexity of drafting applications while enhancing the productivity of drafters. It also has enhanced the nature of drafting by creating more possibilities for design and drafting. As technology continues to advance, employers will look for drafters with a strong background in fundamental drafting principles, a high level of technical sophistication and the ability to apply their knowledge to a broader range of responsibilities.

While growth is expected to be greatest for mechanical, architectural and civil drafters, demand for particular drafting specialties varies throughout the country because employment usually is contingent on the needs of local industry. Employment of drafters remains highly concentrated in industries that are sensitive to cyclical changes in the economy, primarily manufacturing industries. During recessions, drafters may be laid off. However, a growing number of drafters should continue to find employment on a temporary or contract basis as more companies turn to the employment services industry to meet their changing needs.

***Earnings:*** Drafters' earnings vary by specialty, location and level of responsibility. Median annual earnings of architectural and civil drafters were $39,190 in May 2004. The middle 50 percent earned between $31,460 and $47,800. The lowest 10 percent earned less than $25,670 and the highest 10 percent earned more than $57,670. Median annual earnings for architectural and civil drafters in architectural, engineering and related services were $38,760.

Median annual earnings of mechanical drafters were $43,000 in May 2004. The middle 50 percent earned between $34,090 and $54,240. The lowest 10 percent earned less than $27,490 and the highest 10 percent earned more than $67,650. Median annual earnings for mechanical drafters in architectural, engineering and related services were $44,560.

Median annual earnings of electrical and electronics drafters were $43,180 in May 2004. The middle 50 percent earned between $33,920 and $56,110. The lowest 10 percent earned less than $27,600 and the highest 10 percent earned more than $72,050. In architectural, engineering and related services, median annual earnings for electrical and electronics drafters were $42,200.

### *Landscape Architects*

***Significant Points:*** More than 26 percent of all landscape architects are self-employed—more than 3 times the proportion for all professionals.

A bachelor's degree in landscape architecture is the minimum requirement for entry-level jobs; many employers prefer to hire landscape architects who also have completed at least one internship.

Landscape architect jobs are expected to increase due to a growing demand for incorporating natural elements into man-made environments, along with the need to meet a wide array of environmental restrictions.

***Nature of the Work:*** Everyone enjoys attractively designed residential areas, public parks and playgrounds, college campuses, shopping centres, golf courses, parkways and industrial parks. Landscape architects design these areas so that they are not only functional, but also beautiful and compatible with the natural environment. They plan the location of buildings, roads and walkways and the arrangement of flowers, shrubs and trees.

Landscape architects work for many types of organizations—from real estate development firms starting new projects to municipalities constructing airports or parks—and they often are involved with the development of a site from its conception. Working with architects, surveyors and engineers, landscape architects help determine the best arrangement of roads and buildings. They also collaborate with environmental scientists, foresters and other professionals to find the best way to conserve or restore natural resources. Once these decisions are made, landscape architects create detailed plans indicating new topography, vegetation, walkways and other landscaping details, such as fountains and decorative features.

In planning a site, landscape architects first consider the nature and purpose of the project and the funds available. They analyze the natural elements of the site, such as the climate, soil, slope of the land, drainage and vegetation; observe where sunlight falls on the site at different times of the day and examine the site from various angles; and assess the effect of existing buildings, roads, walkways and utilities on the project.

After studying and analyzing the site, landscape architects prepare a preliminary design. To account for the needs of the client as well as the conditions at the site, they frequently make changes before a final design is approved. They also take into account any local, State, or Federal regulations, such as those protecting wetlands or historic resources. In preparing designs, computer-aided design (CAD) has become an essential tool for most landscape architects. Many landscape architects also use video simulation to help clients envision the proposed ideas and plans. For larger scale site planning, landscape architects also use geographic information systems technology, a computer mapping system.

Throughout all phases of the planning and design, landscape architects consult with other professionals, such as civil engineers, hydrologists, or architects, involved in the project. Once the design is complete, they prepare a proposal for the client. They produce detailed plans of the site, including written reports, sketches, models, photographs, land-use studies and cost estimates and submit them for approval by the client and by regulatory agencies.

When the plans are approved, landscape architects prepare working drawings showing all existing and proposed features. They also outline in detail the methods of construction and draw up a list of necessary materials. Landscape architects then mainly monitor the implementation of their design, with general contractors or landscape contractors usually directing the actual construction of the site and installation of plantings.

Some landscape architects work on a variety of projects. Others specialize in a particular area, such as residential development, street and highway beautification, waterfront improvement projects, parks and playgrounds, or shopping centres. Still others work in regional planning and resource management; feasibility, environmental impact and cost studies; or site construction.

Increasingly, landscape architects are becoming involved with projects in environmental remediation, such as preservation and restoration of wetlands or abatement of stormwater run-off in new developments. Historic landscape preservation and restoration is another important area where landscape architects are increasingly playing an important role.

Most landscape architects do at least some residential work, but relatively few limit their practice to individual homeowners. Residential landscape design projects usually are too small to provide suitable income compared with larger commercial or multiunit residential projects. Some nurseries offer residential landscape design services, but these services often are performed by design professionals with fewer formal credentials such as landscape designers, or by others with training and experience in related areas.

Landscape architects who work for government agencies do site and landscape design for government buildings, parks and other public lands, as well as park and recreation planning in national parks and forests.

In addition, they prepare environmental impact statements and studies on environmental issues such as public land-use planning. Some restore degraded land, such as mines or landfills. Other landscape architects use their skills in traffic-calming, the "art" of slowing traffic down through use of traffic design, enhancement of the physical environment and greater attention to aesthetics.

***Working Conditions:*** Landscape architects spend most of their time in offices creating plans and designs, preparing models and cost estimates, doing research, or attending meetings with clients and other professionals involved in a design or planning project. The remainder of their time is spent at the site. During the design and planning stage, landscape architects visit and analyze the site to verify that the design can be incorporated into the landscape. After the plans and specifications are completed, they may spend additional time at the site observing or supervising the construction. Those who work in large national or regional firms may spend considerably more time out of the office travelling to sites away from the local area.

Salaried employees in both government and landscape architectural firms usually work regular hours; however, they may work overtime to meet a project deadline. Hours of self-employed landscape architects vary depending on the demands of the projects on which they are working.

***Training, Other Qualifications and Advancement:*** A bachelor's or master's degree in landscape architecture usually is necessary for entry into the profession. A bachelor's degree in landscape architecture takes 4 or 5 years to complete. There also are two types of accredited master's degree programmes. The most common type of master's degree is a 3-year first professional degree programme designed for students with an undergraduate degree in another discipline.

The second type of master's degree is a 2-year second professional degree programme for students who have a bachelor's degree in landscape architecture and who wish to teach or specialize in some aspect of landscape architecture, such as regional planning or golf course design.

In 2004, 59 colleges and universities offered 77 undergraduate and graduate programmes in landscape architecture that were accredited by the Landscape Architecture Accreditation Board of the American Society of Landscape Architects.

College courses required in these programmes usually include technical subjects such as surveying, landscape design and construction, landscape ecology, site design and urban and regional planning. Other courses include history of landscape architecture, plant and soil science, geology, professional practice and general management.

The design studio is another important aspect of many landscape architecture curriculums. Whenever possible, students are assigned real projects, providing them with valuable hands-on experience. While working on these projects, students become more proficient in the use of computer-aided design, geographic information systems and video simulation.

In 2004, 47 States required landscape architects to be licensed or registered. Licensing is based on the Landscape Architect Registration Examination (LARE), sponsored by the Council of Landscape Architectural Registration Boards and administered in two portions, graphic and multiple choice. Each portion of the testing is conducted over two days.

Admission to the exam usually requires a degree from an accredited school plus 1 to 4 years of work experience under the supervision of a registered landscape architect, although standards vary from State to State. Currently, 14 States require that a State examination be passed in addition to the L.A.R.E. to satisfy registration requirements. State examinations, which usually are 1 hour in length and completed at the end of the L.A.R.E., focus on laws, environmental regulations, plants, soils, climate and any other characteristics unique to the State.

Because State requirements for licensure are not uniform, landscape architects may not find it easy to transfer their registration from one State to another.

However, those who meet the national standards of graduating from an accredited programme, serving 3 years of internship under the supervision of a registered landscape architect and passing the L.A.R.E. can satisfy requirements in most States. Through this means, a landscape architect can obtain certification from the Council of Landscape Architectural Registration Boards and so gain reciprocity (the right to work) in other States.

In the Federal Government, candidates for entry positions should have a bachelor's or master's degree in landscape architecture. The Federal Government does not require its landscape architects to be licensed.

Persons planning a career in landscape architecture should appreciate nature, enjoy working with their hands and possess strong analytical skills. Creative vision and artistic talent also are desirable qualities. Good oral communication skills are essential; landscape architects must be able to convey their ideas to other professionals and clients and to make presentations before large groups. Strong writing skills also are valuable, as is knowledge of computer applications of all kinds, including word processing, desktop publishing and spreadsheets. Landscape architects use these tools to develop presentations, proposals, reports and land impact studies for clients, colleagues and superiors.

The ability to draft and design using CAD software is essential. Many employers recommend that prospective landscape architects complete at least one summer internship with a landscape architecture firm in order to gain an understanding of the day-to-day operations of a small business, including how to win clients, generate fees and work within a budget.

In States where licensure is required, new hires may be called "apprentices" or "intern landscape architects" until they become licensed. Their duties vary depending on the type and size of the employing firm. They may do project research or prepare working drawings, construction documents, or base maps of the area to be landscaped. Some are allowed to participate in the actual design of a project. However, interns must perform all work under the supervision of a licensed landscape architect. Additionally, all drawings and specifications must be signed and sealed by the licensed landscape architect, who takes legal responsibility for the work.

After gaining experience and becoming licensed, landscape architects usually can carry a design through all stages of development. After several years, they may become project managers, taking on the responsibility for meeting schedules and budgets, in addition to overseeing the project design. Later, they may become associates or partners of a firm, with a proprietary interest in the business.

Many landscape architects are self-employed because start-up costs, after an initial investment in CAD software, are relatively low. Self-discipline, business acumen and good marketing skills are important qualities for those who choose to open their own business. Even with these qualities, however, some may struggle while building a client base.

Those with landscape architecture training also qualify for jobs closely related to landscape architecture and may, after gaining some experience, become construction supervisors, land or environmental planners, or landscape consultants.

***Employment:*** Landscape architects held about 25,000 jobs in 2004. Almost 6 out of 10 workers were employed in firms that provide architectural, landscape architectural, engineering and landscaping services. State and local governments were the next largest employers. About 1 out of 4 landscape architects was self-employed.

Employment of landscape architects is concentrated in urban and suburban areas throughout the country; some landscape architects work in rural areas, particularly those employed by the Federal Government to plan and design parks and recreation areas.

***Job Outlook:*** Employment of landscape architects is expected to increase faster than the average for all occupations through the year 2014. In addition to growth, the need to replace landscape architects who retire or leave the labour force will produce some additional job openings. Employment will grow because the expertise of landscape architects will be highly sought after in the planning and development of new residential, commercial and other types of construction to meet the needs of a growing population.

With land costs rising and the public desiring more beautiful spaces, the importance of good site planning and landscape design is growing. In addition, new demands to manage stormwater run-off in both existing and new landscapes, combined with the growing need to manage water resources in the Western States, should cause increased demand for this occupation's services.

New construction also is increasingly contingent upon compliance with environmental regulations, zoning laws and water restrictions, which will spur demand for landscape architects to help plan sites that meet these requirements and integrate new structures with the natural environment in the least disruptive way. Landscape architects also will be increasingly involved in preserving and restoring wetlands and other environmentally sensitive sites.

Continuation of the Transportation Equity Act for the Twenty-First Century also is expected to spur employment for landscape architects, particularly through State and local governments. This Act, known as TEA-21, provides funds for surface transportation and transit programmes, such as interstate highway construction and maintenance and environment-friendly pedestrian and bicycle trails.

In addition to the work related to new development and construction, landscape architects are expected to be involved in historic preservation, land reclamation and refurbishment of existing sites. They are also doing more residential design work as households spend more on landscaping than in the past.

Because landscape architects can work on many different types of projects, they may have an easier time than other design professionals finding employment when traditional construction slows down. Opportunities will vary from year to year and by geographic region, depending on local economic conditions. During a recession, when real estate sales and construction slow down, landscape architects may face greater competition for jobs and sometimes layoffs.

New graduates can expect to face competition for jobs in the largest and most prestigious landscape architecture firms, but should face good job opportunities overall as demand increases, while the number of graduates of landscape architecture holds steady or only goes up slightly. Opportunities will be best for landscape architects who develop strong technical skills—such as computer design—and communication skills, as well as knowledge of environmental codes and regulations.

Those with additional training or experience in urban planning increase their opportunities for employment in landscape architecture firms that specialize in site planning as well as landscape design. Many employers prefer to hire entry-level landscape architects who have internship experience, which significantly reduces the amount of on-the-job training required.

***Earnings:*** In May 2004, median annual earnings for landscape architects were $53,120. The middle 50 percent earned between $40,930 and $70,400. The lowest 10 percent earned less than $32,390 and the highest 10 percent earned over $90,850. Architectural, engineering and related services employed more landscape architects than any other group of industries and there the median annual earnings were $51,670 in May 2004.

In 2005, the average annual salary for all landscape architects in the Federal Government in non-supervisory, supervisory and managerial positions was $74,508.

Because many landscape architects work for small firms or are self-employed, benefits tend to be less generous than those provided to workers in large organizations.

3

# Other Designing Career

## Jewellery Designing

On the back of a sizzling growth of the organised jewellery industry, striking job openings and exciting entry-level salaries, many specialised institutes catering to the industry have mushroomed in the recent past. It's a fine era to consider jewellery designing as a career preference.

India is the largest gems and jewellery market in the world (the domestic market is Rs 63,000 crore), but largely in the unorganised sector with a significant focus on gold. With the entry of big players like Tanishq, Swarovski, DeBeers, D'- damas, the shifting thrust on gems and stones rather than pure gold is giving a big push to the organised gems and jewellery industry.

Your grandma's old jewellery may be treasured and pricey heirlooms, but they simply do not hold a candle to the existing styles being worn. Jewellery these days is exclusive and contemporary. "People are very image cognizant. They don't want jewellery as a representation of financial security but to make a fashion statement and also as trends wear that suits different occasions."

***Getting Started:*** Previously, the single way to learn this skill was to be an apprentice to an experienced jeweller. But these days, one can take up a diploma course in jewellery design after school. Numerous institutes, all over India, present diploma courses in jewellery designing. A student has to pass an aptitude test and interview before qualifying for the course.

One could be from any field. But an art background does help in the long run.

The course gives you essential information on the diverse kinds of stones, colour schemes in jewellery, design themes, presentation and framing, designing individual jewellery pieces, men's jewellery, costume jewellery, jewellery costing, etc. But to a professional in designing jewellery does not need formal training. A professional in any other field can take up jewellery designing workshops and set up a business production house.

*What it Takes?*

- There are no specific personality traits for jewellery designers. One can learn everything while getting trained. However, you just need a passion for the profession; otherwise there is no way one can learn.
- A sense of design is imperative. Precision and attention to detail are also equally important for a successful jeweller. One should be very creative, imaginative and technically sound.
- It's also important to have a working knowledge about manufacturing.
- One should be well-versed with the fashion industry on the international front too.

*The Job...:*

- Jewellery designers prepare sketches—by hand or on the computer—to conceptualise the design. After consulting with the customer or the manufacturing team, designers fashion detail drawings, a structural model, computer simulations, or a full-scale prototype.
- Computer models allow superior effortlessness and flexibility in exploring a number of design alternatives, thus reducing design costs and cutting the time it takes to deliver a product to market.
- Designs are created on regular or floral patterns and then generate forms by connecting different structures together. The range of raw materials is exhaustive—from economical and easily available stuff like paper, wood, terracotta, jute, to highly priced Swarovski crystals!

***Opportunities:*** *One can work in any of the following sectors:*

- Jewellery designing house
- Export house
- Fashion house
- Self-employment
- Freelance designing

If you join an export house, you can see your new designs in the international market. Most of the students start their own business by setting up a production house.

As a freelance designer your job is to draw a design according to the specifications of the jewellers' house. You also need to direct the manufacturing of the jewellery by the craftsman of the jewellery house.

*Where to study..?*

- NIFT Campus, opposite Gulmohar Park, Hauz Khas, New Delhi.
- Srimati Nathibai Damodar Training (SNDT) Women's University, Mumbai.
- Gem and Jewellery Export Promotion Council, Rajasthan Bhavan, Jaipur.
- Jewellery Export Promotion Council, D-15 Commerce Centre, Tardeo, Mumbai.
- Indian Institute of Jewellery, Modern Centre, 101, Sane Guruji Marg, Mahalaxmi, Mumbai.
- Jewellery Design and Technology Institute (JDTI), Noida.
- South Delhi Polytechnic for Women, Lajpat Nagar IV, New Delhi.
- St. Xavier's College, Geology Department, Mumbai.
- Small Industries Service Institute, Chennai.

There are many more reputed institutes in India and abroad imparting expertise in the field of Jewellery Designing!

## Jewellery/Silver Designer

Jewellery/silver designers create designs for jewellery, silverware and other forms of decorative and functional metallic products. Designs may be used for mass production or for handcrafted items.

***Work Activities:*** Jewellery and silver designers create designs for a wide variety of jewellery, silverware and cutlery products.

Most designers begin their careers in industry, designing products for the mass market. They may look at the products their company already makes and see how they can change them to suit new styles and trends.

They may also be asked to design and develop new products. This usually involves the following:

- Looking at products made by their own and competitors' companies.
- Finding out if there are any new ways to make things, or new materials to make them with.
- Thinking about what kind of people are likely to buy the products.

Designers may do this research themselves or with the help of marketing managers. Then they prepare detailed drawings so that craftworkers can make the final product. Different companies use different methods of production. Some combine traditional and 'high-tech' methods. Others may use machines for all steps in the production process.

***Personal Qualities and Skills:*** You will need in-depth knowledge of both traditional and modern production methods. Designers work closely with skilled craftworkers like diamond-mounters, turners, polishers and engravers. You may specialise in one particular area of the trade, such as horology. You need an eye for detail and, if you are also involved in making up jewellery, you need good practical skills.

***Pay and Opportunities:*** Pay rates for jewellery/silver designers vary with employer and responsibilities. The pay rates given below are approximate. Jewellery/silver designers earn in the range of £16,500—£21,000 a year, rising to £29,000—£37,000. Higher earners can make around £40,500 a year. Self-employed designer-craftworkers are likely to earn at the lower end of the range, especially when they start out. Self-employed designer craft-workers are likely to earn at the lower end of the range, especially when they start out.

Jewellery/silver designers work a basic 39-hour week, Monday to Friday. However, late finishes and weekend work may be required, especially as deadlines approach. Self-employed designers may work irregular hours, depending on how much work they have week-to-week.

Employers include firms involved in producing jewellery, silverware and cutlery products. London is regarded as the traditional centre for fine jewellery. Birmingham is home to a wide range of fine jewellery and costume jewellery production, badge making and gold and silver-smithing. Sheffield is famous for its cutlery and silver and steel products.

Some jewellery/silver designers set up as designer craft-workers and work from home or a shared studio. Entry to this area of work is very competitive.

The following information is sourced from government statistics. The government's definition of types of job is slightly different to that used in this programme. For this type of job, the most relevant Government-defined occupation is 'Product, clothing and related designers'.

In 2001 there were 2,600 people working as 'Product, clothing and related designers' in Scotland. 12 in every 10,000 employees working in Scotland were employed as 'Product, clothing and related designers'.

***Entry Routes and Training:*** The usual route into this area of design is to do a degree or Higher National Diploma course in Jewellery or Jewellery and Silversmithing.

Specialist degree courses are available in Scotland at:

- Dundee University: BDes (Hons) Jewellery and Metal Design
- Edinburgh College of Art: BA (Hons) Jewellery and Silversmithing
- Glasgow School of Art: BA (Hons) Design; Silversmithing and Jewellery
- Robert Gordon's University: BA (Hons) Three Dimensional Design

The Goldsmiths' Company provides a number of prizes, bursaries, awards and sponsorship for those studying to enter the craft and industry.

***Qualifications:*** Usual entry requirements for Art and Design courses are:

- some Standard Grades for National Certificate level
- a suitable National Certificate or 1/3 Highers for Higher National Certificate/Higher National Diploma level
- 3 Highers (A-C), normally including English and Art and Design, plus 2 Standard Grades (1-3) for degree level

However, entry requirements vary and alternative qualifications may be accepted—check prospectuses for details.

A central feature of the selection procedure for admission to any course in Art and Design is the submission of a comprehensive portfolio of work that demonstrates the candidate's potential. Entry to all courses is very competitive.

***Adult Opportunities:*** Work experience gained as an assistant in a design studio or workshop is valued. Commercial awareness and an understanding of the jewellery/precious metal industry is an advantage.

Suitable applicants aged 21 or over may do a college or university Access course. No formal qualifications are required to enter an Access course, but you should check individual course details. They lead to relevant degree/HND courses.

Many colleges relax the normal academic entry requirements for applicants with experience in arts, crafts or design.

To enter this work or relevant courses, you need to have a portfolio of work showing your creative ability.

Financial support is available from the South Square Trust for degree level study of silver/jewellery design.

- 51% of people in occupations such as jewellery/silver designer are self-employed.
- 20% work part-time.
- 7% have flexible hours.

## Commercial and Industrial Designers

***Significant Points:*** Commercial and industrial designers usually work closely with engineers, materials scientists, marketing and corporate strategy staff, cost estimators and accountants.

About 1 out of 3 are self-employed.

A bachelor's degree in industrial design, architecture, or engineering is required for entry-level positions; however, many commercial and industrial designers choose to pursue a master's degree in either industrial design or business administration.

Keen competition is expected for most jobs because many qualified individuals are attracted to careers in this field; those with strong backgrounds in engineering and computer-aided design, as well as extensive business expertise, will have the best prospects.

***Nature of the Work:*** Commercial and industrial designers combine the fields of art, business and engineering to design the products used every day by businesses and consumers. These designers are responsible for the style, function, quality and safety of most manufactured goods. Usually these designers will specialize in one particular product category. Some specialties include automobiles and other transportation vehicles, appliances, technology goods, medical equipment, furniture, toys, tools and construction equipment and housewares.

The first steps in developing a new design, or altering an existing one, are to determine the requirements of the client, the ultimate function for which the design is intended and its appeal to customers or users. When creating a new design, designers often begin by researching the product user or the context in which the product will be used and desired product characteristics, such as size, shape, weight, colour, materials used, cost, ease of use, fit and safety. Designers gather this information by meeting with clients, conducting market research, reading design and consumer publications, attending trade shows and visiting potential users, suppliers and manufacturers.

Designers then prepare conceptual sketches or diagrams—by hand or with the aid of a computer—to illustrate the vision for the design. After conducting research and consulting with a creative director or other members of the product development team, designers then create detailed sketches or renderings. Many designers use computer-aided design (CAD) tools to create and better visualize the final product. Computer models allow ease and flexibility in exploring a greater number of design alternatives, thus reducing design costs and cutting the time it takes to deliver a product to market.

Industrial designers who work for manufacturing firms also use computer-aided industrial design (CAID) tools to create designs and machine-readable instructions that communicate with automated production tools. Often, designers will create physical models out of clay, wood and other materials to give clients a better idea of what the finished product will look like.

Designers then present the designs and prototypes to their client or managers and incorporate any changes and suggestions. Designers also will work with engineers, accountants and cost estimators to determine if the product could be made safer, easier to assemble or use, or cheaper to manufacture. Designers also may participate in usability and safety tests with prototypes in order to make further adjustments to the design before it goes to manufacturing.

Commercial and industrial designers also work with marketing staff to develop plans to best market the new product or design to consumers. Increasingly, designers are working with corporate strategy staff to ensure that their designs fit into the company's business plan and strategic vision. This involves designing new products that accurately reflect the company's image and values. It also involves identifying and designing products that best fit consumers' needs before a competitor markets a similar product. Increasingly, designers must focus on creating innovative products in addition to considering the style and technical aspects of the product.

***Working Conditions:*** Working conditions and places of employment vary. Designers employed by manufacturing establishments, large corporations, or design firms generally work regular hours in well-lighted and comfortable settings. Designers in smaller design consulting firms, or those who freelance, may work on a contract, or job, basis. They frequently adjust their workday to suit their clients' schedules and deadlines, meeting with the clients during evening or weekend hours when necessary. Consultants and self-employed designers tend to work longer hours and in smaller, more congested, environments. Additional hours may be required in order to meet deadlines.

Designers may transact business in their own offices or studios or in clients' homes or offices. They also may travel to other locations, such as testing facilities, design centres, clients' exhibit sites, user's homes or workplaces and manufacturing facilities. With the increased speed and sophistication of computers and advanced communications networks, designers may form international design teams, serve a geographically more dispersed clientele, research design alternatives by using information on the Internet and purchase supplies electronically.

***Training, Other Qualifications and Advancement:*** A bachelor's degree in industrial design, architecture, or engineering is required for most entry-level commercial and industrial design positions. Many candidates in industrial design also pursue a master's degree in order to increase their employment opportunities. Creativity and technical knowledge are crucial in this occupation. People in this field also must have a strong sense of the esthetic—an eye for colour and detail and a sense of balance and proportion. Designers must understand the technical aspects of how the product functions. Despite the advancement of computer-aided design, sketching ability remains an important advantage. A good portfolio—a collection of examples of a person's best work—often is the deciding factor in getting a job.

Bachelor's of fine arts or bachelor's of science degrees in industrial design are granted at many colleges and universities and in private art and design schools. Baccalaureate curriculum includes principles of design, sketching, computer-aided design, industrial materials and processes, manufacturing methods and some coursework in engineering, physical science, mathematics, psychology and anthropology. Many programmes also include internships in design or manufacturing firms.

Commercial and industrial designers also may pursue a master's degree in industrial design. With the growing emphasis on strategic design and how products fit into the overall business plan, an increasing number of designers are pursing a master's degree in business administration in order to gain valuable business skills. Also, a growing number of professionals in other industries, such as marketing and information technology, are entering the industrial design field by pursuing advanced degrees in design.

The National Association of Schools of Art and Design accredits about 250 post-secondary institutions with programmes in art and design. Approximately 45 of these schools award a degree in industrial design. Many schools require the successful completion of 1 year of basic art and design courses before formal entry into a bachelor's degree programme. Applicants also may be required to submit sketches and other examples of their artistic ability.

Employers increasingly expect new designers to be familiar with computer-aided design software as a design tool. Designers must also be creative, imaginative and persistent and must be able to communicate their ideas in writing, visually and verbally. Because tastes in style can change quickly, designers need to be well read, open to new ideas and influences and quick to react to changing trends. Problem-solving skills and the ability to work independently and under pressure also are important traits. People in this field need self-discipline to start projects on their own, to budget their time and to meet deadlines and production schedules.

As strategic design becomes more important, employers will seek designers with project management skills and knowledge of accounting, marketing, quality assurance, purchasing and strategic planning. Good business sense and sales ability also are important, especially for those who freelance or run their own business.

Beginning commercial and industrial designers usually receive on-the-job training and normally need 1 to 3 years of training before they can advance to higher level positions. Experienced designers in large firms may advance to chief designer, design department head, or other supervisory positions. Some designers leave the occupation to become teachers in design schools or in colleges and universities. Many faculty members continue to consult privately or operate small design studios to complement their classroom activities. Some experienced designers open their own design firms.

***Employment:*** Commercial and industrial designers held about 49,000 jobs in 2004. About 1 out of 3 were self-employed. About 13 percent of designers were employed in either engineering or specialized design services firms. Manufacturing companies employed the rest of commercial and industrial designers, with the largest number employed in aerospace products and parts manufacturing.

***Job Outlook:*** Employment of commercial and industrial designers is expected to grow about as fast as average for all occupations through 2014. Employment growth will arise from an expanding economy and from an increase in consumer and business demand for new or upgraded products. However, competition for jobs will be keen because many talented individuals are attracted to the design field. The best job opportunities will be in specialized design firms which are used by manufacturers to design products or parts of products. Designers with strong backgrounds in engineering and computer-aided design, as well as extensive business expertise, may have the best prospects.

Increasing demand for commercial and industrial designers will stem from the continued emphasis on the quality and safety of products, the increasing demand for new products that are easy and comfortable to use and the development of high-technology products in consumer electronics, medicine, transportation and other fields. However, employment can be affected by fluctuations in the economy. For example, during periods of economic downturns, companies may cut research and development spending, including new product development.

Increasingly, manufacturers have been outsourcing design work to design services firms in order to cut costs and to find the most qualified design talent. Additionally, some companies use design firms located overseas, especially for design of high-technology products. These overseas design firms are located closer to their suppliers, which reduces the time it takes to design and sell a product—an important consideration when technology is changing quickly. Offshoring of design work, particularly for high-technology products, could continue to have a negative impact on domestic employment of commercial and industrial designers.

Despite the increase in design work performed overseas, most design jobs—particularly jobs not related to high-technology product design—will still remain in the U.S. because design is essential to a firm's success and firms will want to retain control over the design process. As the demand for design work becomes more consumer-driven, designers also will need to closely monitor and react to, changing customer demands. Designers will increasingly have to come up with innovative new products in order to stay competitive. Domestic designers also will be required to work with marketing and strategic planning staffs to design products that will be more usable and appealing to consumers and that accurately define a company's image and brand.

***Earnings:*** Median annual earnings for commercial and industrial designers were $52,310 in May 2004. The middle 50 percent earned between $39,130 and $68,980. The lowest 10 percent earned less than $29,080 and the highest 10 percent earned more than $86,250.

## Floral Designers

***Significant Points:*** Job opportunities should be good because of relatively high replacement needs stemming from low starting pay and limited advancement opportunities.

Floral design is the only design specialty that does not require formal post-secondary training.

Many floral designers work long hours on weekends and holidays, filling orders and setting up decorations for weddings and other events.

About 1 out of 3 is self-employed.

***Nature of the Work:*** *Floral designers*, or florists, cut live, dried, or silk flowers and other greenery and arrange them into displays of various sizes and shapes. They design these displays by selecting flowers, containers and ribbons and arranging them into bouquets, corsages, centerpieces of tables, wreaths and the like for weddings, funerals, holidays and other special occasions. Some floral designers also utilize accessories such as balloons, candles, toys, candy and gift baskets as part of their displays.

Job duties can vary by type of employment setting. Most floral designers work in small independent floral shops that specialize in custom orders and also handle large orders for weddings, caterers, or interior designers. Floral designers may meet with customers to discuss the arrangement or work from a written order. They note the occasion, the customer's preferences, the price of the order, the time the floral display or plant is to be ready and the place to which it is to be delivered. For special occasions, floral designers usually will help set up floral decorations. Floral designers also will prearrange a few displays to have available for walk-in customers or last-minute orders. Some floral designers also assist interior designers in creating live or silk displays for hotels, restaurants and private residences.

Some florists work in the floral departments of grocery stores or for Internet florists, which specialize in creating prearranged floral decorations and bouquets. These floral retailers also may fill small custom orders for special occasions and funerals, but some grocery store florists do not deliver to clients or handle large custom orders. Florists who work for wholesale flower distributors assist in the selection of different types of flowers and greenery to purchase and sell to retail florists. Wholesale floral designers also select flowers for displays that they use as examples for retail florists.

Self-employed floral designers must handle the various aspects of running their own businesses, such as selecting and purchasing flowers, hiring and supervising staff and maintaining financial records. Self-employed designers also may run gift shops or wedding consultation businesses in addition to providing floral design services. Some conduct design workshops for amateur gardeners or others with an interest in floral design.

***Working Conditions:*** Most floral designers work in comfortable, well-lit spaces in retail outlets or at home, although working outdoors is sometimes required. Designers also may frequently make short trips delivering flowers, setting up arrangements for special events and procuring flowers and other supplies.

Floral designers have frequent contact with customers and must work to satisfy their demands, including last-minute holiday and funeral orders. Because many flowers are perishable, most orders cannot be completed too far in advance. As a result, some designers often work long hours before and during holidays. Some also work nights and weekends to complete large orders for weddings and other special events.

Floral designers may suffer muscle strain from long periods of standing and from repeated finger and arm movements required to make floral arrangements. They are susceptible to back strain from lifting and carrying heavy flower arrangements. Designers also may suffer allergic reactions to certain types of pollen when working with flowers. In addition, they frequently use sharp objects—scissors, knives and metal wire—that can cause injuries if handled improperly.

***Training, Other Qualifications and Advancement:*** Floral design is the only design occupation that does not require formal post-secondary training; most floral designers learn their skills on the job. Employers generally look for high school graduates who have creativity, a flair for arranging flower and a desire to learn. Many florists gain their initial experience working as cashiers or delivery people in retail floral stores. The completion of formal design training, however, is an asset for floral designers, particularly those interested in advancing to chief floral designer or in opening their own businesses.

Private floral schools, vocational schools and community colleges award certificates in floral design. These programmes generally require a high school diploma for admission and last from several weeks to 1 year. Floral design courses teach the basics of arranging flowers—the different types of flowers there are, their colour and texture, cutting and taping techniques, tying bows and ribbons, proper handling and care of flowers, floral trends and pricing.

Some floral designers also may choose to attend an associate's or bachelor's degree programme at a community college or university. Some programmes offer formal degrees in floral design, while others offer degrees in floriculture, horticulture, or ornamental horticulture, which can prepare students for a career in floral design. In addition to floral design courses, these programmes teach courses in botany, chemistry, hydrology, microbiology, pesticides and soil management.

Since many floral designers manage their own business, additional courses in business, accounting, marketing and computer technology can be helpful.

The American Institute of Floral Designers offers an accreditation examination as an indication of professional achievement in floral design. The exam consists of a written part covering floral terminology and an onsite floral-arranging test in which candidates have 4 hours to complete five floral designs. The five categories of floral designs are funeral tributes, table arrangements, wedding arrangements, wearable flowers and in one category of the candidate's choosing.

Floral designers must be creative, service oriented and able to communicate their ideas visually and verbally. Because trends in floral design change quickly, designers must be open to new ideas and react quickly to changing trends. Problem-solving skills and the ability to work independently and under pressure also are important traits. Individuals in this field need self-discipline to budget their time and meet deadlines.

Advancement in the floral field is limited. After a few years of on-the-job training, designers can either advance to a supervisory position or open their own floral shop.

***Employment:*** Floral designers held about 98,000 jobs in 2004. Approximately 1 out of 3 was self-employed. Almost half of all floral designers worked in florist shops. Another 8 percent worked in the floral departments of grocery stores. Others were employed by miscellaneous nondurable goods merchant wholesalers, other general merchandise stores and in lawn and garden equipment and supply stores.

***Job Outlook:*** Employment of floral designers is expected to grow about as fast as average for all occupations through 2014. Job opportunities should be good because of the relatively high replacement needs in retail florists that result from comparatively low starting pay and limited opportunities for advancement.

The demand for floral designers will continue to grow as flower sales increase as a result of the increasing population and lavishness of weddings and other special events that require floral decorations. As disposable incomes rise, more people also desire fresh flowers in their homes and offices. Increased spending on interior design also is creating demand for stylish artificial arrangements for homes and businesses.

Opportunities should be available in grocery store and Internet floral shops as sales of floral arrangements from these outlets grow. The prearranged displays and gifts available in these stores appeal to consumers because of the convenience and because of prices that are lower than can be found in independent floral shops.

As mass marketers capture more of the small flower orders, independent floral shops are increasingly finding themselves under pressure to remain profitable. Many independent shops have added online ordering systems in order to compete with Internet florists. Others are trying to distinguish their services by specializing in certain areas of floral design or by combining floral design with event planning and interior design services. Some florists also are adding holiday decorating services in which they will set up decorations for businesses and residences.

Few job opportunities are expected in floral wholesalers, primarily because an increasing number of shops are purchasing flowers and supplies directly from growers in order to cut costs. In addition, the growth of e-commerce in the floral industry will make it easier for retail florists to locate their own suppliers.

***Earnings:*** Median annual earnings for wage and salary floral designers were $20,450 in May 2004. The middle 50 percent earned between $16,670 and $25,610. The lowest 10 percent earned less than $14,360 and the highest 10 percent earned more than $32,370. Median annual earnings were $22,520 in grocery stores and $20,110 in florists.

## Jewellers and Precious Stone and Metal Workers

***Significant Points:*** About 40 percent of all jewellers are self-employed.

Jewellers usually learn their trade in vocational or technical schools, through distance-learning centres, or on the job.

Prospects for new jewellers should be excellent; many employers have difficulty finding and retaining workers with the right skills to replace those who retire or who leave the occupation for other reasons.

***Nature of the Work:*** Jewellers and precious stone and metal workers use a variety of common and specialized handtools and equipment to design and manufacture new pieces of jewellery; cut, set and polish gem stones; repair or adjust rings, necklaces, bracelets, earrings and other jewellery; and appraise jewellery, precious metals and gems.

Jewellers usually specialize in one or more of these areas and may work for large jewellery manufacturing firms, for small retail jewellery shops, or as owners of their own businesses. Regardless of the type of work done or the work setting, jewellers require a high degree of skill, precision and attention to detail.

Some jewellers design or make their own jewellery. Following their own designs or those created by designers or customers, they begin by shaping the metal or by carving wax to make a model for casting the metal.

The individual parts then are soldered together and the jeweller may mount a diamond or other gem or may engrave a design into the metal. Others do finishing work, such as setting stones, polishing, or engraving. Typical repair work includes enlarging or reducing ring sizes, resetting stones and replacing broken clasps and mountings.

In larger manufacturing businesses, jewellers usually specialize in a single operation. *Mold and model makers* create models or tools for the jewellery that is to be produced. *Assemblers* solder or fuse jewellery and their parts; they also may set stones. *Engravers* etch designs into the metal with specialized tools and *polishers* bring a finished luster to the final product.

Jewellers typically do the handiwork required to produce a piece of jewellery, while *gemologists* and laboratory graders analyze, describe and certify the quality and characteristics of gem stones. Gemologists may work in gemological laboratories or as quality control experts for retailers, importers, or manufacturers. After using microscopes, computerized tools and other grading instruments to examine gem stones or finished pieces of jewellery, they write reports certifying that the items are of a particular quality. Many jewellers also study gemology in order to become familiar with the physical properties of the gem stones with which they work.

Jewellery *appraisers* carefully examine jewerly to determine its value, after which they write appraisal documents. They determine the value of a piece by researching the jewellery market, using reference books, auction catalogues, price lists and the Internet. They may work for jewellery stores, appraisal firms, auction houses, pawnbrokers, or insurance companies. Many gemologists also become appraisers.

In small retail stores or repair shops, jewellers and appraisers may be involved in all aspects of the work. Those who own or manage stores or shops also hire and train employees; order, market and sell merchandise; and perform other managerial duties.

New technology is helping to produce jewellery of higher quality at a reduced cost and in a shorter amount of time. For example, lasers are often used for cutting and improving the quality of stones, for applying intricate engraving or design work and for inscribing personal messages or identification on jewellery. Jewellers also use lasers to weld metals together in milliseconds with no seams or blemishes, improving the quality and appearance of jewellery.

Some manufacturing firms use computer-aided design and manufacturing (CAD/CAM) to facilitate product design and automate some steps in the mold-making and modelmaking process. CAD allows jewellers to create a virtual-reality model of a piece of jewellery. Using CAD, jewellers can modify the design, change the stone, or try a different setting and see the changes on a computer screen before cutting a stone or performing other costly steps.

Once they are satisfied with the model, CAM produces it in a waxlike or other material. After the mold of the model is made, it is easier for manufacturing firms to produce numerous copies of a given piece of jewellery, which are then distributed to retail establishments across the country. Similar techniques may be used in the retail setting, allowing individual customers to review their jewellery designs with the jeweller and make modifications before committing themselves to the expense of a customized piece of jewellery.

***Working Conditions:*** A jeweller's work involves a great deal of concentration and attention to detail. Working on precious stones and metals while trying to satisfy customers' and employers' demands for speed and quality can cause fatigue or stress. However, the use of more ergonomically correct jewellers' benches has eliminated most of the strain and discomfort caused by spending long periods bending over a workbench in one position.

Lasers require both careful handling to avoid injury and steady hands to direct precision tasks. In larger manufacturing plants and some smaller repair shops, chemicals, sharp or pointed tools and jewellers' torches pose safety threats and may cause injury if proper care is not taken. Most dangerous chemicals, however, have been replaced with synthetic, less toxic products to meet safety requirements.

In repair shops, jewellers usually work alone with little supervision. In retail stores, they may talk with customers about repairs, perform custom design work and even do some selling. Because many of their materials are valuable, jewellers must observe strict security procedures, including working behind locked doors that are opened only by a buzzer, working on the other side of barred windows, making use of burglar alarms and, in larger jewellery establishments, working in the presence of armed guards.

***Training, Other Qualifications and Advancement:*** Jewellers usually learn their trade in vocational or technical schools, through distance-learning centres, or on the job. Colleges and art and design schools offer programmes that can lead to the degree of bachelor of fine arts, or master of fine arts, in jewellery design. Formal training in the basic skills of the trade enhances one's employment and advancement opportunities. Many employers prefer jewellers with design, repair and sales skills.

For those interested in working in a jewellery store or repair shop, vocational and technical training or courses offered by public and private colleges are the best sources of training. In these programmes, which can vary in length from 6 months to 1 year, students learn the use and care of jewellers' tools and machines and basic jewellry-making and jewellery-repairing skills, such as designing, casting and setting and polishing stones.

Technical school courses also cover topics such as blueprint reading, math and shop theory. To enter some technical school programmes and most college programmes, a high school diploma or its equivalent is required. However, some schools specializing in jewellery training do not require graduation from high school. Computer-aided design is being used increasingly in the jewellery field and students—especially those interested in design and manufacturing—may wish to obtain training in CAD; however, most employers will provide such training.

Various institutes offer courses and programmes in gemology. Programmes cover a wide range of topics, including the identification and grading of diamonds and gem stones.

Most employers feel that vocational school and technical school graduates need up to a year of additional supervised on-the-job training or apprenticeship in order to refine their repair skills and learn more about the operation of the store or shop.

In addition, some employers encourage workers to improve their skills by enrolling in short-term technical school courses such as fabricating, jewellery design, jewellery manufacturing, wax carving and gemology. Employers may pay all or part of the cost of this additional training.

In jewellery manufacturing plants, workers traditionally develop their skills through informal apprenticeships and on-the-job training. The apprenticeship or training period lasts up to 1 year, depending on the difficulty of the specialty. Training usually focuses on casting, setting stones, making models, or engraving. In recent years, a growing number of technical schools have begun to offer training designed for jewellers working in manufacturing. Employers in manufacturing may prefer graduates of these programmes because they are familiar with the production process, requiring less on-the-job training.

The precise and delicate nature of jewellery work requires finger and hand dexterity, good hand-eye coordination, patience and concentration. Artistic ability and fashion consciousness are major assets, because jewellery must be stylish and attractive. Those who work in jewellery stores have frequent contact with customers and should be neat, personable and knowledgeable about the merchandise. In addition, employers require workers of good character, because jewellers work with valuable materials.

Advancement opportunities are limited and depend greatly on an individual's skill and initiative. In manufacturing, some jewellers advance to supervisory jobs, such as master jeweller or head jeweller, but for most, advancement takes the form of higher pay for doing the same job. Jewellers who work in jewellery stores or repair shops may become managers; some open their own businesses.

Those interested in starting their own business should first establish themselves and build a reputation for their work within the jewellery trade. Once they obtain sufficient credit from jewellery suppliers and wholesalers, they can acquire the necessary inventory. Also, because the jewellery business is highly competitive, jewellers who plan to open their own store should have sales experience, as well as knowledge of marketing and business management. Courses in these areas often are available from technical schools and community colleges.

***Employment:*** Jewellers and precious stone and metal workers held about 42,000 jobs in 2004. About 40 percent of these workers were self-employed; many operated their own store or repair shop and some specialized in designing and creating custom jewellery.

About 1 out of 5 jobs for jewellers and precious stone and metal workers were in other miscellaneous manufacturing, which includes jewellery and silverware manufacturing. Another 3 out of 10 jobs were in retail trade, primarily in jewellery, luggage and leather goods stores. A small number of jobs were with merchant wholesalers of miscellaneous durable goods and in repair shops providing repair and maintenance of personal and household goods. Although jewellery stores and repair shops were found in every city and in many small towns, most jobs were in larger metropolitan areas. In 2004, many jewellers employed in manufacturing worked in Rhode Island, New York, or California.

***Job Outlook:*** Employment of jewellers and precious stone and metal workers is expected to **decline** slightly through 2014. Employment opportunities, however, should be excellent. New jewellers will be needed to replace those who retire or who leave the occupation for other reasons. When master jewellers retire, they take with them years of experience that require substantial time and financial resources to replace. Many employers have difficulty finding and retaining jewellers with the right skills and the necessary knowledge. Some technological advances have made jewelrymaking more efficient; however, many tasks cannot be fully automated. Jewellery work is a labour-intensive process that requires excellent handiwork.

The increasing numbers of affluent individuals, working women, double-income households and fashion-conscious men are expected to keep jewellery sales strong. The population aged 45 and older, which accounts for a major portion of jewellery sales, also is on the rise.

Non-traditional jewellery marketers, such as discount stores, mail-order and catalogue companies, television shopping networks and Internet retailers, have expanded the number of buying options and increased their sales volume. However, these establishments require fewer sales staff, limiting employment opportunities for jewellers and precious stone and metal workers who work mainly in sales. Because such establishments enjoy increases in sales, however, they will need highly skilled jewellers to make and repair the jewellery they sell.

Opportunities in jewellery stores and repair shops will be best for graduates from training programmes for jewellers or gemologists. Despite an increase in sales by non-traditional jewellery marketers, traditional jewellers should not be affected greatly, because they have the advantage of being able to build client relationships based on trust. Many clients prefer to work directly with a jeweller, to ensure that the product is of the highest quality and meets their specifications. Many traditional jewellers expand their businesses as clients recommend their services to friends and relatives.

The jewellery industry can be cyclical. During economic downturns, demand for jewellery products and for jewellers tends to decrease. However, demand for repair workers should remain strong even during economic slowdowns, because maintaining and repairing jewellery is an ongoing process. In fact, demand for jewellery repair may increase during recessions, as people repair or restore existing pieces rather than purchase new ones. Also, many non-traditional vendors typically do not offer repair services.

Within manufacturing, increasing automation will adversely affect employment of low-skilled occupations, such as assemblers and polishers. Automation will have a lesser impact on more creative, highly skilled positions, such as moldmakers and modelmakers. Furthermore, small manufacturers, which typify the industry, will have an increasingly difficult time competing with the larger manufacturers when it comes to supplying large retailers.

Because of recent international trade agreements, exports are increasing modestly as manufacturers become more competitive in foreign markets. However, imports from foreign manufacturers are increasing more rapidly than exports, due to these same agreements. Imports compete mainly with mass-produced jewellery. Therefore, employment in luxury and custom jewellery manufacturing is least susceptible to decline caused by import competition.

***Earnings:*** Median annual earnings for jewellers and precious stone and metal workers were $27,400 in May 2004. The middle 50 percent earned between $20,510 and $37,280. The lowest 10 percent earned less than $16,040 and the highest 10 percent earned more than $49,020. In May 2004, median annual earnings in the industries employing the largest numbers of jewellers and precious stone and metal workers were $30,530 in jewellery, luggage and leather goods stores and $23,590 in other miscellaneous manufacturing.

Most jewellers start out with a base salary, but once they become more proficient, they may begin charging by the number of pieces completed. Jewellers who work in retail stores may earn a commission for each piece of jewellery sold. Many jewellers also enjoy a variety of benefits, including reimbursement from their employers for work-related courses and discounts on jewellery purchases.

## Drafting and Design Technology

Drafting and design technology programmes prepare people to draw plans for architects, engineers and others. Students learn to use drafting machines, CAD programmes and drawing tools. They also learn to make calculations, estimate materials and make blueprints.

Every product we use and every structure we live and work in started out as a design. This is true for a house, a machine, a toy, a chair, or an electronic circuit. And every design had to be represented by a drawing—a draft—so that the people who constructed the product would know what to make.

Drafting and design used to be very separate tasks. A designer would make a freehand sketch of a concept, or maybe construct a crude model using cardboard, putty and scrap materials. Then, a drafter would take that sketch or model and create drawings of exactly what a finished product would look like. The drawings would show the product from several different angles. Then, the designer would ask for changes and the drafter would have to tear up the drawings and start over again.

Nowadays the two processes are closer together. Designers may still start with crude sketches or models, but often they are able to create a crude representation of the design using computer-assisted drafting and design (CADD) software. Then, it is the drafter's job to refine that CADD representation. Using CADD, the drafter and designer can rotate the image in three dimensions and view it from every possible angle. If something needs to be changed, the drafter merely modifies the design rather than starting from scratch.

When you study drafting and design technology, you still learn the principles of drawing by hand and with tools. But much of the focus is on using CADD.

You also have to learn one or more of the fields that use drafts. For example, some programmes specialize in architectural drafting. In such a programme, you would also study architectural terms and the problems of design and engineering that architects face. You would learn how to estimate needs for building materials from the details of a design. You would learn how to create and read blueprints.

On the other hand, if your programme emphasized drafting for manufacturing, you would learn different subjects. You would learn what aspects of a design make something easy or hard to manufacture. You would learn at least the rudiments of how to turn the draft into computer code that controls the machine tools that do the manufacturing.

Most educational programmes in this field take about two years of full-time study beyond high school. Many community or two-year colleges and technical institutes offer this programme. Although the schools are different, often the programmes are very similar. Keep in mind that you may want to get more education later. A four-year college is more likely to give you credit for courses taken at a community college."

### *College Preparation*

You can prepare for this programme of study by completing your high school degree or getting a GED.

*Business Computer Applications*

*Drafting*

*Algebra*

### *Typical Course Work*

An associate degree programme in this field typically includes courses in the following subjects:

- Advanced CADD Programming and Customization
- Algebra and Trigonometry
- Architectural Drafting
- Civil Drafting
- Computer Presentation and Animation
- Computer-Assisted Drafting and Design (CADD)
- Electromechanical Systems
- Electronics Drafting
- Fundamentals of Machining
- Introduction to Computers
- Mechanical/Industrial Drafting
- Technical Communication

### *Things to Know*

Even if you never enter another degree programme, you will need to keep learning over the course of your career. Computer technology will continue to change and new drafting software will be developed. You will need to take courses to keep your skills up-to-date.

You may want to consider becoming certified by the American Design Drafting Association (ADDA). Employers usually do not require this. Nevertheless, it can show that you have a good understanding of standard drafting concepts and practices. To be certified, you need to pass an exam.

Graphic, Interior, Fashion and Industrial Design Careers, Jobs and Training Design Career and Job Highlights.

One of the chief benefits of being a designer is that a very large number, almost one third, of all designers are self-employed. That is almost five times the percentage of self-employed people in other fields. Also, many people are attracted to designing because of the high level of creativity it demands. Generally to be a designer you need at least a bachelor's degree and a master's degree will be advantageous. The industry is showing signs of growth, but there is still very high competition for most projects, as there are many extremely talented and creative designers.

***The Design Profession:*** Designers are innately creative people. They then make use of their creativity, artistry and knowledge of practical skills to turn their creative vision into plans for our Websites, clothes, advertisements, cars, media and surroundings. Since designers are needed in so many industries they usually generalize, focusing on one specialized area like interior design, cars, company logos, newspapers, clothing, theatre sets, merchandise displays, medical equipment, or many others. To be a good designer you have to take three things into account: 1) What your client needs and has the resources for, 2) The primary function of the design and 3) How it will appeal to customers. Often the first step is solid research of the preferred design characteristics like cost, safety issues, availability of materials, size, etc.

The next step is to prepare a preliminary outline, such as a sketch, usually with the aid of a computer. You will then share your creative vision with the client or a product development team. Next comes a detailed plan of your design, including very detailed drawings or blueprints, simulations, or a to-scale model. More and more designers are using CAD (Computer-Aided Design) to increase efficiency, create a better model and because computers make it easier to explore new possibilities and design permutations. Computers are becoming more popular because they allow for greater creativity while cutting costs. Industrial designers create designs and instructions that are readable by machines and that give directions to automated production tools using CAD's sister tool, CAID (Computer-Aided Industrial Design).

Many designers are also involved in the business aspects of their job, not jut the creative. They often have assistants to supervise. Also, many designers own their own business and so they have to be involved in client development, networking, finding and renting space, ordering materials, reviewing industry publications and many other administrative responsibilities. Furthermore, as technology in computers and communication advances, designers need to continually work to stay up-to-date and competitive.

This is especially true for those designers involved in industrial or graphic design. Computers have allowed for great advancements in the design industry. Advanced communications networks have increased the opportunities that were previously limited by geography. Designers can form international firms or taskforces and can work for clients all over the world. The Internet has increased the availability of information, making research easier and better and designers have a much larger pool of supplies. This makes the logistics of being a self-employed designer much easier, as well.

### *Types of Designers*

There are many types of designers who work in a wide range of industries. Some designers generalize and work in many different fields, while others concentrate on one specialty.

- *Commercial / Industrial Design:* This area helps develop manufactured products, such has automobiles, airplanes, computers, kitchen appliances, medical equipment, automobile interiors, office materials, etc. In addition to their creativity and artistry, a successful commercial designer has to be able to assess the needs of user and have a working knowledge of marketing and means of production. All of these skills are necessary to create an effective, appealing product. Commercial and industrial designers tend to specialize in an area like home appliances or recreational equipment.
- *Fashion Design:* This deals with designing apparel. Many are self-employed in the form of clothing labels and many work for personal clients. Others work for particular

boutiques or department stores. These fashion designers are very creative and innovative, while others stick to established trends for high-demand items. However, these small, self-employed designers are in the minority. The majority of fashion designers work for big clothing manufactures, making clothing and accessories for the mass market.

- *Floral Design:* This is a very diverse area, with many working in large shops and others working for themselves in very small, specialized shops. All floral designers, however, are involved in arranging all types of flowers into designs. They make arrangements based on the customer's order for all occasions, from wedding bouquets to holiday wreaths, from tabletop gardens to large terrariums. Aside from the artistic side of floral design, designers also have to be competent in assessing the customer's needs, the type of occasion, the availability and cost of flowers according to season, materials of imitation flowers and issues of time and delivery to make sure the flowers look their best. Also, in small flower shops many designers also have to do their own accounting and arrange supply and delivery, which requires business know-how. Many floral designers also grow their own flowers, which expands their responsibilities even further.
- *Graphic Design:* This is an extremely large area of design. Basically, graphic designers resolve communication problems using visual solutions. By studying culture, context and social issues they develop designs that will effectively communicate to meet the needs of their customer. They use a number of media, from print to computers to film and so many graphic designers specialize in one area. Some have expertise in visual layout for magazines or computers, others create promotional displays, others design the credits for movies and others design logos, others design signs for the government. There are many areas of specialization. Computers are instrumental in almost all areas of graphic design, however, especially in the ever-growing technological industry: designing Web pages and multimedia projects.

- *Interior Design:* The perennial goal of interior designers is to combine from and function. They improve the quality of interior spaces by increasing efficiency, safety and beauty. Interior designers can work on all types of projects, like residential homes, shopping malls, retail stores, hospitals, hotels, theaters, or restaurants. With such a wide range of work, most interior designers specialize, for example one designer might focus on businesses while another might focus on residences. Many specialize in even more specific areas, like airplane interiors or kitchens. A successful designer has to take many things into account, like the customer's preferences, cost of materials and functional efficiency. Also, there are many federal and local guidelines and building codes. Plus, if designing a public space, it is necessary to ensure that everything is accessible to the disabled and elderly. Keeping all those in mind, a designer then configures the interior structure, such as molding, windows and built-in fixtures; furnishings, such as furniture and floor coverings; lighting that is economical and pleasing; and accents like rugs and wall-hangings. They coordinate colours, styles and materials to create a visually pleasing and comfortable space. Computers are extremely useful to interior designers as they allow for exact and accurate models and also allow for easy adjustments to the whims of customers.
- *Visual Merchandise Design:* Also called window-dressing, visual merchandize design is the art of merchandise display. Many designers work for large businesses, arranging merchandise in retail stores or designing window displays. Working for the interior of retail stores involves dressing mannequins, creating table displays, arranging props and accents and organizing clothing placement by colour group or style. To make promotions and styles uniform and to maintain the "look" of a store, most large retail chains employ designers at the corporate level in a central design department. The designs are distributed to individual stores and individual managers

or regional designers adapt the designs to meet individual needs.

- *Set Design:* This area of design makes sets and exhibits for movie and television studios, theatre productions, or special exhibitions in museums or trade-shows. Designers who work with television or theatre need to study scripts and consult with writers and directors to ensure that their design is in line with their artistic vision. They also need to research make sure their design is historically accurate in architectural details and fashion. They then provide the models for the actual construction, making sure that it is feasible and functional. Designers of special exhibitions need to confer with museum curators or trade-show sponsors to make use of the available space, create an effective theme and control flow of human traffic. Also, if working for a museum a designer may have to consult an art specialist to ensure preservation and security of museum objects.

***Working Conditions:*** Designers face many pressures in their work. They are creative people by nature and so they often don't have traditional office environments. They may work in their own home or in that of their client. They often travel to the location of their work, whether it is a showroom, a client's house, or an office under construction. Many designers do not have fixed incomes but are paid by project, which creates pressures to finish a job quickly and get new clients. Further frustrations are caused when designs are rejected or don't turn out as planned and sometimes creativity just doesn't seem to come.

Designers may work at many different places under many different conditions. Manufactures, large design firms, or corporations usually make for a very stable working environment in terms of regular and reasonable hours in a comfortable office setting. Designers who work freelance or who work at small firms usually work according to whatever individual contract they have at the time, making adjustments to their client's need, which makes for a less stable environment. They may have uneven working hours, with varying workloads and more evening and weekend hours. Designers who are self-employed or who work as consultants often work longer hours in a smaller and simpler offices.

Hours and conditions depend not only on the type of firm, but also on the type of designer. Industrial and graphic designers and interior designers generally work quite regular hours, but may have to work extra hours or weekends to meet the demands of a particular project.

Set and exhibit designers, however, often have much more uneven schedules, working long hours under pressure and having to make quick adjustments. Fashion designers often operate the same way, having to work very long hours in preparation for a fashion show, or travelling to the site of a show. Floral designers mostly work regular hours in small, agreeable working conditions but large events like wedding may require some extra hours.

Merchandise designers may work regular hours in a corporate job, but those who work in actual retail stores often have irregular hours as they do most of their work when customers are out of the store. Also many designers, especially those in interior, merchandise and fashion design, have to deal with equipment transportation, sample books, heavy displays, supervising construction and many other responsibilities.

***Becoming a Designer:*** Though different types of designers require different personalities and skill sets, creativity is common to all designers. It is necessary for designers to seek for beauty and balance and have a sense of the aesthetic. Also, since they spend so much time dealing with customers and complex projects, they have to have good communication skills and analytical thinking that leads to problem-solving. And even though computers have had such an impact on designing, most designers, especially those in fashion, have some kind of artistic training that enable them to make sketches and plans.

The amount of schooling needed depends on the type of design. However, it is important to keep in mind that schooling isn't always the deciding factor in getting a job. A sampling of a designer's work in the form of a portfolio is usually the most important.

Fashion designers generally have an associate's degree or bachelor's degree from a reputable fashion design college. It is also imperative that a potential fashion designer be conversant in patterns, accessories, trends, fabrics and the fashion industry as a whole. Set and exhibit designers usually have 4-year degrees as well and often a Masters in Fine Arts as well. An important credential for set designers is membership in the United Scenic Artists, Local 829.

For floral designers, many people enter the profession by gaining on-the-job experience rather than formal schooling. Professionals look for trainees, generally people with at least a high school degree who are eager to learn and very artistic. However, formal schooling is beneficial, especially for people who want to own their own businesses or hold a management position. Many vocational schools offer short (less than a year) courses in floral design. Community colleges and universities often offer associate's and bachelor's degrees in horticulture, floral design, ornamental horticulture. Also, to become an accredited floral designer, a potential designer needs to pass an examination given by the American Institute of Floral Designers.

Two and three-year programmes at professional schools are also offered for many other types of design. Degrees from such programmes usually qualify graduates to become assistants to designers. Four-year programmes at colleges and universities supply graduates with a Bachelor of Fine Arts Degree. These degrees involve a more rigorous and varied curriculum, involving mechanical drawing, sketching, art history, design principles and other skills applicable to the various areas of design. Most designers, especially those who want to work independently, are recommended to find programmes that have a strong liberal arts core that will teach business management, marketing, psychology and art. Also, architectural skills can be very helpful to designers, especially those in interior design.

The National Association of Schools of Art and Design offer many design degrees in areas like art, interior design, industrial design, graphic design and fashion design. They accredit over 200 schools, many of which require at least a year of studying basic design and art before admitting students to the bachelor's degree programme. Admission to the programme may also require a portfolio of samples and sketches.

Another professional organization for designers is the Foundation for Interior Design Education Research. They also offer bachelor's degrees in the areas of architecture, art and home economics in over 120 schools and programmes.

Though most designers have some formal schooling, fledgling designers receive a lot of hands-on experience in the first few years of their career. This experience is very important for them to gain promotions to positions of more responsibility like chief designer or department head. They may even establish their own firm. Many designers, after a few years of experience, work in 3academia as professors at design schools or universities. Many of these continue to be involved in "fieldwork", however, as consultants or freelance designers.

***Industry and Job Outlook:*** As they economy expands, more people are demanding the skills of designers and analysts anticipate growth for the industry. Competition for positions, however, will continue to be fierce, as there are many gifted and competent people who want to be designers. Ingenuity, persistence and more formal schooling will set apart those who will succeed.

Graphic design has the highest projected growth rate. As more businesses look to the Interned Web for information and as the entertainment market (including television, video games, movies and advertisements) expands, there is more and more call for graphic designers.

There is also increasing demand for interior designers, especially for offices, retail stores, homes and establishments specializing in care for the elderly. Floral design has a relatively high turnover rate due to a lack of advancement opportunities, which leads to new jobs.

The area of industrial design will continue to grow rapidly as the importance of safety and quality of products grows. As customers want everything to be cheaper, more comfortable, easier to use and as technology becomes more important in every field, industrial design is a very important industry. A few areas of design, however, do not show this rapid growth. New jobs for merchandise displayers will come from the natural turnover caused by workers who retire or move to different professions. The industry of clothing manufacturing is slowing, which means that growth in fashion design is also slowing. And the area of exhibit and set designing is very small, so even though there is a lot of growth there will not be a lot of job openings.

## Furniture Designer

*Also known as:* Designer, Furniture.

Furniture designers create designs for mass-produced and handcrafted furniture products. They must consider the function of an item of furniture and the limitations of the material that it's made from, (*e.g.*, wood, metal or plastic) as well as the way it looks.

***Work Activities:*** Furniture designers create designs for mass-produced and handcrafted furniture products. The most common products they are required to design are those that are found in homes and offices, such as chairs, tables and bookcases.

The first stage is to put together a design brief. This helps the designer to establish a client's requirements. They need to know the type of furniture they need, its function, what type of person the product is to appeal to and the budget available. Discussions with clients are necessary in order to establish these facts. In large companies, in-house designers usually receive the design brief from senior management or marketing departments.

Before any designs can be produced, furniture designers need to investigate the designs that are already in the market place, how well these designs are selling and customers' reactions to the existing products. This stage often involves collecting and analysing market research.

When they have completed their research, furniture designers make rough sketches. Once senior management and/

or clients have approved these, designers produce more detailed drawings that show the dimensions of the product and any written instructions. The designer may have to prepare mock-ups and prototypes of products to show other people what the product looks like and how well it stands up to wear and tear.

Self-employed designer-craftworkers carry out all these tasks themselves. They usually rely on commissions from individuals who want original one-off pieces of furniture made to their specific requirements. To produce the finished item, the designer-craftworker often uses traditional craft methods. This can involve using a range of equipment, such as hand tools, lathes and machine saws. It requires skills in techniques such as veneering, wood turning, carving, wood finishing and upholstery.

***Personal Qualities and Skills:*** As a furniture designer, you will need to be:

- Artistic and inventive.
- Flexible enough to adapt your designs to suit company house styles and clients' requirements.
- Able to work creatively and logically through the design process, seeking original and practical solutions to design problems.
- Aware of the production possibilities and limitations of materials that are used to manufacture furniture products, for example wood, metal and plastic.

Practical craft skills are especially important for self-employed designer-craftworkers, as are business skills. Communication and presentation skills are especially important when dealing with clients and when managing projects.

***Pay and Opportunities:*** Pay rates for furniture designers vary with employer and responsibilities. The pay rates given below are approximate. Furniture designers earn in the range of £16,500—£21,000 a year, rising to £29,000—£37,000. Higher earners can make around £40,500 a year. Self-employed designer-craftworkers are likely to earn at the lower end of the range, especially when they start out. Some designers negotiate royalties for their designs with manufacturers.

Furniture designers work a basic 39-hour week, Monday to Friday. Working hours for self-employed designers may be irregular, depending on how much work they have. However, late finishes and weekend work may be required from time to time, especially as deadlines approach.

Employers include firms involved in large-scale furniture production that may employ furniture designers as part of an in-house design team, or employ freelance designers. Other opportunities can be found with design consultancies where designers work with other professionals in related fields, for example interior designers and architects. Some furniture designers set up as designer craft-workers and work from home or a shared studio or workshop. Entry to furniture design is very competitive.

The following information is sourced from government statistics. The government's definition of types of job is slightly different to that used in this programme. For this type of job, the most relevant Government-defined occupation is 'Product, clothing and related designers'.

In 2001 there were 2,600 people working as 'Product, clothing and related designers' in Scotland. 12 in every 10,000 employees working in Scotland were employed as 'Product, clothing and related designers'.

***Entry Routes and Training:*** Most furniture designers have a degree in Furniture Design or Three-Dimensional Design (of which furniture design is an option).

A central feature of admission to any course in Art and Design is the submission of a comprehensive portfolio of work that demonstrates the candidate's potential.

Edinburgh College of Art offer a degree in Design and Applied Arts (Furniture & Product Design).

***Qualifications:*** Usual entry requirements for Art and Design courses are:

- some Standard Grades for National Certificate level
- a suitable National Certificate or 1/3 Highers for Higher National Certificate/Higher National Diploma level
- 3 Highers (A-C), normally including English and Art and Design, plus 2 Standard Grades (1-3), for degree level

However, entry requirements vary between courses and alternative qualifications may be accepted—check prospectuses for details.

A central feature of the selection procedure for admission to any course in Art and Design is the submission of a comprehensive portfolio of work that demonstrates the candidate's potential.

Entry to all courses is very competitive.

***Adult Opportunities:*** Work experience gained as an assistant in a design studio or workshop is valued. Commercial awareness and an understanding of the furniture manufacturing industry is an advantage.

Suitable applicants aged 21 or over may do a college or university Access course. No formal qualifications are required to enter an Access course, but you should check individual course details. They lead to relevant degree/HND courses.

Many colleges relax the normal academic entry requirements for applicants with experience in arts, crafts or design.

To enter this work or relevant courses, you need to have a portfolio of work showing your creative ability.

The Worshipful Company of Furniture Makers offers training opportunities in the form of short tours and courses for design, manufacturing and retail newcomers to the industry. Applications are made via company or academic department.

- 51% of people in occupations such as furniture designer are self-employed.
- 20% work part-time.
- 7% have flexible hours.

## Product Designer

Product designers create designs for three-dimensional objects ranging from domestic products such as kettles, hairdryers and washing machines, to industrial appliances.

***Work Activities:*** Product designers create designs for manufactured, three-dimensional products. They are interested in the aesthetic aspects of the product (the way it looks), but also consider the purpose, materials, costs, technical specifications and methods of production. The type of products they design can range from domestic appliances such as radios, television sets and food processors, to large industrial machine tools.

Working to a brief, the designer carries out detailed research before producing a series of drawings and sketches that can be refined and modified to create a model or prototype. If this is accepted, the designer can make further changes to the design before turning it into a final working drawing for production staff to follow.

Most product designers begin as design assistants, gradually improving their design skills before becoming design managers or consultants. They work closely with design and production engineers, who offer technical advice and help turn design ideas into plans and working models. They also work with marketing managers, who brief the designer on the type of person or audience they want the product to appeal to.

Freelance product designers may have administrative duties as well as their usual design responsibilities. These may include arranging meetings with clients or potential employers, negotiating contracts and marketing products.

***Personal Qualities and Skills:*** As a product designer, you must have good practical art and design skills. Your drawings need to be clear, precise and well presented. In most cases designers use computer-aided design (CAD) systems to help them. You also need good communication skills, as you will spend a lot of time in discussions and meetings with both clients and colleagues.

You need good eyesight and normal colour vision.

***Pay and Opportunities:*** Pay rates for product designers vary with the industry and responsibilities. The pay rates given below are approximate. Product designers earn in the range of £16,500—£21,000 a year, rising to £29,000—£37,000. Higher earners can make around £40,500 a year.

Product designers work a basic 39-hour week, Monday to Friday. Working hours for self-employed designers may be irregular, depending on how much work they have. Late finishes and weekend work may be required from time to time, especially as deadlines approach. Employers throughout the UK are large manufacturing companies and design consultancies. Some experienced designers work on a freelance basis.

The following information is sourced from government statistics. The government's definition of types of job is slightly different to that used in this programme. For this type of job, the most relevant Government-defined occupation is 'Product, clothing and related designers'.

In 2001 there were 2,600 people working as 'Product, clothing and related designers' in Scotland. 12 in every 10,000 employees working in Scotland were employed as 'Product, clothing and related designers'.

***Entry Routes and Training:*** Choosing a relevant degree course can be quite confusing as product design straddles the areas of both art and science. Because of this, relevant courses are offered as BA, BSc, BEng and MEng degrees.

However, BSc and BEng/MEng degrees have different entry requirements and are usually aimed at those who want to become design engineers. These courses normally ask for Highers in both Maths and Physics/Technological Studies. You will still need artistic ability.

Entry requirements for BA degrees are the same as other design courses. It is also possible to enter this work with a Higher National Diploma in product design.

Professional bodies such as the Chartered Society of Designers (CSD) and the Design Business Association (DBA) offer relevant training courses and professional development opportunities.

***Qualifications:*** Entry to BSc and BEng/MEng degrees normally requires Higher passes in Maths and Physics/ Technological Studies. These courses are primarily aimed at people who want to become design engineers.

There are a number of routes into Higher National Diplomas or degrees in Design, via Standard Grades and Highers or through suitable National Certificate courses.

However, entry requirements vary between courses and alternative qualifications may be accepted—check prospectuses for details.

***Adult Opportunities:*** Work experience gained as an assistant in a design studio or workshop or in a design consultancy is valued. Experience in related fields, such as advertising or marketing, is also useful. Commercial awareness and an understanding of the industry you wish to work is an advantage.

Suitable applicants aged 21 or over may do a college or university Access course. No formal qualifications are required to enter an Access course, but you should check individual course details. They lead to relevant degree/HND courses.

Many colleges relax the normal academic entry requirements for applicants with experience in arts, crafts or design. To enter this work or relevant courses, you will normally need to have a portfolio of work showing your creative ability.

- 51% of people in occupations such as product designer are self-employed.
- 20% work part-time.
- 7% have flexible hours.

## Packaging Designer

Also known as: Designer, Packaging

Packaging designers create designs for containers such as bottles, cartons and boxes. In addition to design talent, packaging designers also need to understand the capabilities of packaging materials.

***Work Activities:*** Packaging designers create designs for all forms of packaging including bottles, cartons and boxes. Their designs must be versatile enough to protect and preserve the contents of the package and look good enough to persuade people to buy the product.

They work on their ideas using traditional design tools such as pens and paints and, often, computer-aided design (CAD). Meetings with clients and colleagues also take up a considerable amount of a packaging designer's time.

Once the designer has an idea of what their clients require they make a series of rough sketches, the best of which are refined and presented to the customers for approval. The designer must be prepared to keep changing their design ideas if they do not suit production processes, the clients' product image, or marketing requirements. When the best ideas have been chosen, packaging designers use model making techniques to see what their design looks like in three-dimensional form before it is finalised and before production begins.

***Personal Qualities and Skills:*** As a packaging designer, you will need to know how to use a wide range of packaging materials such as tin, glass, plastic and card. You will also need an understanding of production processes and how your designs affect the environment, for example when packaging is thrown away.

***Pay and Opportunities:*** Pay rates for packaging designers vary with employer and responsibilities. The pay rates given below are approximate. Packaging designers earn in the range of £15,000—£18,000 a year, rising to £24,000—£30,500. Higher earners can make around £40,000 a year.

Packaging designers work a basic 39-hour week, Monday to Friday. However, late finishes and weekend work may be required, especially as deadlines approach.

Most packaging designers work for manufacturing companies as part of an in-house design team, or for a design consultancy. It may also be possible to work for a manufacturing company that specialises in packaging design. Entry to this area of work is very competitive.

The following information is sourced from government statistics. The government's definition of types of job is slightly different to that used in this programme. For this type of job, the most relevant Government-defined occupation is 'Product, clothing and related designers'.

In 2001 there were 2,600 people working as 'Product, clothing and related designers' in Scotland. 12 in every 10,000 employees working in Scotland were employed as 'Product, clothing and related designers'.

***Entry Routes and Training:*** The majority of packaging designers have a degree or Higher National Diploma in a relevant subject such as Graphic Design or Three-Dimensional Design.

***Qualifications:*** Usual entry qualifications for Art and Design courses are:

- Some Standard grades for National Certificate level
- A suitable National Certificate or 1/3 Highers for Higher National Certificate/Higher National Diploma level
- 3 Highers (A-C), normally including English and Art and Design, plus 2 Standard Grades (1-3), for degree level.

However, entry requirements vary between courses and alternative qualifications may be accepted—check prospectuses for details.

A central feature of the selection procedure for admission to any course in Art and Design is the submission of a comprehensive portfolio of work that demonstrates the candidate's potential. Entry to all courses is very competitive.

***Adult Opportunities:*** Work experience gained as an assistant in a design studio or workshop, or in a design consultancy is valued. Experience in related fields, such as advertising or marketing, is also useful. Commercial awareness and an understanding of the packaging industry is an advantage.

Suitable applicants aged 21 or over may do a college or university Access course. No formal qualifications are required to enter an Access course, but you should check individual course details. They lead to relevant degree/HND courses.

Many colleges relax the normal academic entry requirements for applicants with experience in arts, crafts or design.

To enter this work or relevant courses, you need to have a portfolio of work demonstrating your creative ability.

- 20% of people in occupations such as packaging designer work part-time.
- 7% have flexible hours.
- 0% of employees work on a temporary basis.

## Ceramic Pottery Maker

Ceramic pottery makers work mainly in large commercial potteries. They make different types of pottery using traditional craft skills and mechanised processes. Most pottery makers specialise in a particular job, *e.g.*, throwing or casting.

***Work Activities:*** Ceramic pottery makers use a combination of traditional craft skills and mechanised processes to make pottery products. Traditional hand tools are still used in many instances, as this remains the most effective method of manufacture, but automatic tools are often used as they speed up the process. Some of the methods employed by ceramic pottery makers are set out below.

The most common traditional manufacturing process is 'throwing' a pot. A pottery maker throws a lump of clay onto a wheel. This is shaped by hand and by the speed of the wheel, which is controlled by a foot pedal.

'Jiggering' is a mechanised process used to make flatware, such as saucers. The clay is flattened by a thin metal spreader to form a 'batt' of the required thickness. The batt is then removed and thrown onto a rotating plaster mould. This is then either sprayed or wetted by hand and a metal profile tool is pulled down to shape the ware.

'Jolleying' is a mechanised process used to make hollowware, such as soup bowls. The clay is thrown onto a rotating mould, which is then eased up at the sides by hand. A profile tool is brought down to shape the ware. The mould is then placed into a drying cupboard.

'Turning' is a finishing process where the turner operates a rotating machine called a lathe, on which the work has been placed. The ware is shaped using hand or automatic tools.

'Casting' is a process where liquid clay or 'slip' is poured into moulds. The excess moisture is absorbed leaving a coating of clay within. Items may be cast in sections, which the caster will assemble, using slip as the bonding agent. This process is known as 'sticking up'.

***Personal Qualities and Skills:*** Good hand skills are essential in this type of work, especially for throwers and turners. Considerable care and a feel for clay are important, as is the ability to handle delicate ware with confidence.

Patience is required when moulding clay. Creativity and a good eye for detail and design are essential if you are making original items.

***Pay and Opportunities:*** Pay rates for ceramic pottery makers vary depending whether they are employed as an operative in a factory environment or as a craftsperson engaged in hand made pottery in a workshop or studio. The pay rates given below are approximate. Broadly, pottery makers earn in the range of £240—£290 a week, rising to £350—£420. Higher earners can make around £490 a week.

Pottery makers who work in a factory normally work a basic 39—hour week, which may involve shift work and overtime. Craftspeople may work full time, but there may also be opportunities for part-time work.

Employment is mainly in large commercial potteries. There is a concentration of large firms in north Staffordshire. There is also scope for throwers and casters throughout the country in premises with other craftspeople.

Some craftspeople decide to become self-employed. They may set up their own pottery, or share premises with other craftspeople.

The following information is sourced from government statistics. The government's definition of types of job is slightly different to that used in this programme. For this type of job, the most relevant government-defined occupation is 'Glass and ceramics makers, decorators and finishers'.

In 2001 there were 1,400 people working as 'Glass and ceramics makers, decorators and finishers' in Scotland. 6 in every 10,000 employees working in Scotland were employed as 'Glass and ceramics makers, decorators and finishers'.

***Entry Routes and Training:*** Training is generally on the job, firstly by observing an experienced worker to learn basic techniques. You will then advance to making simple shapes while under supervision. The amount of time you spend training largely depends upon the technique you are learning and your ability. Some techniques, such as casting, can be learned in six to twelve weeks. Others, such as throwing or jiggering, can take much longer.

***Qualifications:*** Formal qualifications are not usually needed for entry to this work. However, some Standard Grades including English, Maths and Technological Studies may be useful.

***Adult Opportunities:*** Applicants with some work experience in manufacturing industry have an advantage.

Experience of using your hands in a skilled way is important.

Some artistic ability is needed for certain jobs.

- 29% of people in occupations such as ceramic pottery making are self-employed.
- 11% work part-time.
- 11% have flexible hours.
- 6% work on a temporary basis.

## Model Maker

Model makers build models or 'mock-ups' to help designers gain a better idea of what their design looks like, how it fits into its surroundings and how practical it is. They work with a variety of materials such as wood, plastic and metal.

***Work Activities:*** Model makers build models or 'mock-ups' to help designers get a better idea of what their design looks like, how it fits into its surroundings and how practical the design is. Designers need to see or test their design before a decision is made to spend money and time on its production. If a model shows it does not serve the purpose for which it is designed, this can save its producers a lot of money. Another reason to use models is that non-technical people understand them more easily than complicated technical diagrams. Model making is sometimes called design representation.

After talking to the designer, model makers work from design drawings, plans, photographs or computer graphics. They use materials like wood, plastic, metal, plaster, paper or card to produce models. Machine and hand tools are used to shape the materials. For models with moving parts, basic electronics or mechanical techniques may be used. Painting may also be necessary.

A model can be scaled up or down depending upon what it represents and its purpose. A planned motorway flyover system, for example, will be greatly scaled down, whereas a newly discovered molecular structure will be scaled up. Intricate models may take many months to complete. Models are also used to create special effects in films, television, theatre and in certain types of exhibition.

***Personal Qualities and Skills:*** As a model maker, you will require a combination of creative, technical and practical skills. These skills are often self-taught. You will need patience, accuracy and an ability to pay attention to detail and meet project deadlines. Craft skills and intricate working are important, as is the ability to work well with a range of materials.

***Pay and Opportunities:*** Pay rates for model makers vary depending on the industry and whether they are employed or self-employed. The pay rates given below are approximate. Model makers earn in the range of £18,500—£20,500 a year, rising to £25,000—£29,000. Higher earners can make around £34,500 a year.

Model makers usually work a basic 39-hour week, Monday to Friday. Working hours for self-employed model makers may be irregular, depending on how much work they have. Late finishes and weekend work may be required from time to time, especially as deadlines approach.

Although some model makers work for an employer, most are self-employed, moving from project to project. Work is most likely to be found in civil engineering, architecture, film and television, shipbuilding, motor car manufacture and town planning.

Career progression is limited by a lack of career structure. It is quite a competitive area of work to enter.

The following information is sourced from government statistics. The government's definition of types of job is slightly different to that used in this programme. For this type of job, the most relevant Government-defined occupation is 'Pattern makers (moulds)'. In 2001 there were 100 people working as 'Pattern makers (moulds)' in Scotland. 1 in every 10,000 employees working in Scotland were employed as 'Pattern makers (moulds)'.

***Entry Routes and Training:*** The usual route towards a career as a model maker is to complete a suitable degree or Higher National Diploma course.

Courses in model making at National Qualification and Higher National Certificate/Higher National Diploma level are available at Glasgow Metropolitan College.

There are no degree courses in modelmaking in Scotland. However, there is a range of specialist courses available in England.

Some professional model makers have learned model making skills through a hobby. General craft, design and technology courses may also contain elements of training in model making.

***Qualifications:*** For entry to the National Qualification course in Model Making at Glasgow Metropolitan College, no formal qualifications are required. Entry requirements for the Higher National Certificate/Higher National Diploma course are: a National Qualification or 2 Highers (A-C) and 3 Standard Grades (1-3). The subjects at Higher Grade should include English and Art and Design or Product Design.

Usual entry requirements for Art and Design courses are:

- some Standard Grades for National Certificate or National Qualification level
- a suitable National Qualification/Certificate or 1/3 Highers for Higher National Certificate/Higher National Diploma level
- 3 Highers (A-C), normally including English and Art and Design, plus 2 Standard Grades (1-3), for degree level.

However, entry qualifications vary between courses and alternative qualifications may be acceptable—check prospectuses for details.

A central feature of the selection procedure for admission to any course in art and design is the submission of a portfolio of work showing the candidate's creative ability. Entry to all courses is very competitive.

***Adult Opportunities:*** Knowledge of the wider industry in which you may be working, for example, architecture, town planning or civil engineering can be useful.

The normal entry requirements for training courses may be relaxed for suitable adult candidates with experience in crafts, design or technology.

Applicants will be expected to provide a portfolio of work showing creative ability.

- 16% of people who work in occupations such as model maker are self-employed.

## Picture Framer

Picture framers mount and make frames for pictures and other display items. They prepare frame surrounds using a variety of tools and materials. They cut mounts and assemble pictures according to customers' requirements.

***Work Activities:*** Picture framers make frames for all types of pictures, mirrors and other display items, such as photographs, tapestries, medals and natural specimens. They also mount the pictures or items.

Framers advise customers on the types of frames available and suitable styles. They usually have a selection of mouldings for frames from which customers can choose. They also advise customers on colours and proportions for mounts and the shape of the opening, such as oval, square or rectangular.

Preparation for picture framing involves making careful measurements of the frame, glass, mount and backboard, so that displays are centred and corners are square. Picture framers use a variety of hand tools, such as tenon saws, light hammers, screwdrivers, cutting knives and guillotines.

To make square and rectangular frames, framers measure and cut four strips of picture moulding and then cut the ends at an angle of 45 degrees (this is called a mitre cut). These are joined together usually with an underpinner. Some framers buy in ready-made frames from suppliers, especially round and oval frames. Assembling the picture involves fixing it to the mount, polishing the glass, securing both into the frame with a backing board and then affixing hanging rings.

Self-employed framers work out costs, buy in materials, keep records and manage a workshop.

***Personal Qualities and Skills:*** You will need good practical skills in order to use a variety of hand tools and equipment. It is essential that you make accurate measurements, work neatly and pay attention to detail.

You need normal eyesight and colour vision. You should not be allergic to dust or any of the adhesives used.

An interest in art and design is useful and creative ideas are helpful when talking to customers about presentation.

It is helpful to have a driving licence.

Most framers are self-employed so business skills are necessary. It is important for self-employed framers to communicate well with customers and sell their services effectively.

***Pay and Opportunities:*** The pay rates given below are approximate. Picture framers earn in the range of around £5.10—£6.40 an hour.

Full-time picture framers usually work a basic 39—hour week. Overtime and Saturday work may be required.

Employers throughout the UK are large art and framing companies and shops and galleries. Some picture framers are self-employed. Experienced picture framers may also teach; either on a part-time basis, during the day, or in the evening.

Mature entrants are often artists who carry out framing to supplement their income.

The following information is sourced from government statistics. The government's definition of types of job is slightly different to that used in this programme. For this type of job, the most relevant government-defined occupation is 'Furniture makers, other craft woodworkers'.

In 2001 there were 2,300 people working as 'Furniture makers, other craft woodworkers' in Scotland. 11 in every

10,000 employees working in Scotland were employed as 'Furniture makers, other craft woodworkers'.

***Entry Routes and Training:*** There are no set entry routes into this type of work.

If you find work with an established picture framer you are likely to be taken on as a trainee and learn on the job. It may take several months before you are competent enough to undertake the full range of duties.

Many of the picture framers who set themselves up in a small business learn by attending evening classes or short courses. Some are self-taught through reading books and practising framing as a hobby.

Framers may take tests to qualify as a Guild Commended Framer. This qualification is offered by the Fine Art Trade Guild.

***Qualifications:*** You do not need formal qualifications to enter this work. Standard Grades in subjects such as Art or Technological Studies may be useful.

***Adult Opportunities:*** Many entrants are adults with experience in woodworking of some type.

It is possible to study picture framing by attending local college evening classes or short courses. A keen interest in art and design is important. Practical work experience using your hands is helpful.

- 40% of people in occupations such as picture framing are self-employed.
- 9% of people in occupations such as picture framing work part-time.
- 5% have flexible hours.

## Glass Designer

Also known as: Designer, Glass

Glass designers are specialist craft or product designers working in three main areas: studio glass, architectural glass and stained glass. Their aim is to design functional, reliable and cost effective products for manufacture.

***Work Activities:*** Glass designers are specialist craft or product designers working in three main areas: studio glass, architectural glass and stained glass. In studio and stained glass work, designers are likely to be directly involved in the production or assembly of pieces. In the case of studio work this will often be on a self-employed basis. Glass designers working in architectural glass are product designers, where there is much less direct involvement in actual production processes.

In all forms of glass work, designers are likely to develop ideas and make decisions on the use of appropriate materials and production processes after taking costs into account. The aim is to design functional, reliable and cost effective products for manufacture. Occasionally designers must compromise their ideas to satisfy clients' wishes or because the available resources do not suit the specifications of the manufacturing process.

Studio glass work involves the design and production of decorative and functional glassware items, usually on a small or medium scale. Often these items will be of high quality. Methods such as blowing, casting, slumping (bending), engraving, decorating and texturing are used to manufacture small objects or ornaments. The techniques employed are traditional, although the introduction of modern technology is having an effect on craft production methods. Glassware may be decorated, for example by using high speed rotating wheels and sandblasting.

Architectural glass is manufactured using mass production methods. This includes the design and manufacture of products such as windows, lighting and architectural panels. These products are designed with a particular function in mind, although decoration and appearance will also play a part in development.

Stained glass is a specialist and highly skilled area of design. Most designers are employed on renovation projects, or decorative design for new or existing buildings.

***Personal Qualities and Skills:*** As a glass designer you must be able to visualise products and use shape and colour to good effect. This requires creativity. In addition, you need an interest in and understanding of the technical processes involved in glass production. You must also be able to communicate your ideas in the form of sketches or models.

Designs must be practical as well as pleasing to look at. This is particularly true in the design of architectural glass products. You must, therefore, have an appreciation of the functional aspects of your work.

Deadlines and strict budgets often apply, so an ability to work within these is important. If you are self-employed, you will need well developed business skills, particularly in selling.

***Pay and Opportunities:*** Pay rates for designers vary with employer and responsibilities. Glass designers earn in the range of £15,000—£18,000 a year, rising to £24,000—£30,500. Higher earners can make around £40,000 a year. Self-employed designer-craftworkers are likely to earn at the lower end of the range, especially when they start out.

Glass designers work a basic 39-hour week, Monday to Friday. However, late finishes and weekend work may be required, especially as deadlines approach. Self-employed designers may work irregular hours, depending on how much work they have week-to-week.

Employers include high volume glass product manufacturing companies and specialist design consultancies. They may also employ freelance designers. Some glass designers set up as designer craft-workers and work from home or a shared studio.

Entry to this area of work is very competitive.

The following information is sourced from government statistics. The government's definition of types of job is slightly different to that used in this programme. For this type of job, the most relevant Government-defined occupation is 'Product, clothing and related designers'.

In 2001 there were 2,600 people working as 'Product, clothing and related designers' in Scotland. 12 in every 10,000 employees working in Scotland were employed as 'Product, clothing and related designers'.

***Entry Routes and Training:*** If you are seeking employment with a manufacturing company, you should undertake a degree or Higher National Diploma that includes glass design. These are often three-dimensional or combined design courses. Glass design is commonly studied with ceramics design.

Alternatively, there are craft glass making courses available in some colleges. These cover glassblowing, decoration, handforming and lathe working. These courses may be suitable for designers who hope to become self-employed.

***Qualifications:*** Usual entry requirements for Art and Design courses are:

- some Standard Grades for National Certificate level
- a suitable National Certificate or 1/3 Highers for Higher National Certificate/Higher National Diploma level
- 3 Highers (A-C), normally including English and Art and Design, plus 2 Standard Grades (1-3), for degree level

However, entry requirements vary between courses and alternative qualifications may be accepted—check prospectuses for details.

A central feature of the selection procedure for admission to any course in Art and Design is the submission of a comprehensive portfolio of work that demonstrates the candidate's potential. Entry to all courses is very competitive.

***Adult Opportunities:*** Work experience gained as an assistant in a design studio or workshop, or in a design consultancy is valued. Commercial awareness and an understanding of the glass manufacturing industry is an advantage.

Some people gradually develop a hobby in glass making into a career by selling pieces of glassware they have designed and made themselves.

Most people who enter glass design by this route do so part time while working in other jobs because of the costs of developing a commercial workshop.

Suitable applicants aged 21 or over may do a college or university Access course. No formal qualifications are required to enter an Access course, but you should check individual course details. They lead to relevant degree/HND courses.

Many colleges relax the normal academic entry requirements for applicants with experience in arts, crafts or design.

To enter the work or relevant courses, you need to have a portfolio of work showing your creative ability.

The Worshipful Company of Glaziers and Painters of Glass run competitions and awards to encourage the careers of young artists and craftsmen under 30 years old.

- 51% of people in occupations such as glass designer are self-employed.
- 20% work part-time.
- 7% have flexible hours.

## Craft Designer

Also known as: Designer, Craft

Craft designers create designs for a wide range of two-dimensional and three-dimensional objects. They may work for large-scale manufacturers or be self-employed. Specialisms include: textiles, ceramics, wood, silver/jewellery and glass. Self-employed designers usually make their own products whereas in-house designers usually supervise production.

***Work Activities:*** Craft designers design a broad range of two- and three-dimensional products. Most specialise in a particular area, such as:

- textiles
- ceramics
- wood including furniture
- metalwork/jewellery
- glass
- graphic crafts such as calligraphy and printmaking
- toys
- musical instruments
- embroidery
- leatherwork.

Within each of these areas, some designers produce designs for large-scale production by manufacturers, while others work as designer-craftworkers producing designs on a small scale.

In industry, craft designers are often based in a drawing office. Designer-craftworkers usually work from studios or workshops and are responsible for the whole design process from creating original designs to making and usually selling the craft products. They may make small batches of a range of items or one-off items. Some of these individual pieces are artistic creations that could be considered more as fine art than commercial craft design.

In large scale production, designers work to a brief that outlines the type of product required and how much money is available for production. It also outlines what the product is to be used for and who is likely to use it. Designers then research all aspects of the product. They look at existing or similar products, what types of materials they could use and other technical considerations such as whether the material chosen is suited to the purpose of the product. For example, is it strong enough? Designers then produce sketches and drawings to show different designs, aspects of the products, artistic impressions and technical details. Once designs are accepted, development can involve producing samples or working models and testing a limited run on the production line. Knowledge of the relevant manufacturing process is essential.

Most designer-craftworkers follow a similar design process. They work to a brief and undertake research for commissioned work from clients. Some make studio pieces, which they sell through galleries, craft fairs or their own studios.

Designer-craftworkers produce their finished pieces individually rather than on a production line. They may use traditional skills and techniques, such as handloom weaving, throwing pots, hand-building ceramics and wood carving. Designer-craftworkers are also usually responsible for selling their own work and running their businesses.

***Personal Qualities and Skills:*** To succeed in a career in craft design you need the following skills and qualities:

- Creativity and artistic skills.
- An appreciation of colour, shape and form.
- The imagination and ability to create attractive, saleable pieces of work.
- An individual approach to solving design problems.
- Drawing ability.
- The practical skills needed to use tools and equipment.
- A steady hand and the patience to do fine, detailed work is required for some crafts, such as freehand painting (ceramics) or making delicate jewellery.
- Presentation and communication skills.

In industry, craft designers need a high level of technical understanding, of production capabilities, properties of materials and decorative techniques, for example. It is essential that you keep up-to-date with changes in manufacturing methods and materials, as well as fashion trends and styles.

As a designer-craftworker you will need good business skills to undertake costing and pricing, sales and marketing and book-keeping.

***Pay and Opportunities:*** Pay rates for craft designers vary widely depending on the branch of the industry they are involved in, whether they are employed or self-employed and the reputation of their product. The pay rates given below are approximate.

Broadly, craft designers earn in the range of £15,000—£18,000 a year, rising to £24,000—£30,500. Higher earners can make around £40,000 a year. However, home or studio-based craft designers may earn considerably less than these rates, especially when they start out.

Designers usually work a basic 39-hour week, Monday to Friday. Working hours for self-employed designers may be irregular, depending on how much work they have. However, late finishes and weekend work may be required from time to time, especially as deadlines approach.

Employers include firms involved in the production of textiles, ceramics, wood and metal/jewellery. Opportunities may be found throughout the country in most sectors, although there are concentrations of manufacturers of some products, such as ceramics in North Staffordshire and jewellery in Birmingham and London. Some manufacturers recruit freelance craft designers for certain projects.

There are opportunities for designer craft-workers to set up in urban and rural areas throughout the UK, although it may be more difficult to become established in some areas. Some self-employed designers work from home, or from studios or workshops, which they might share with other designer craft-workers. Entry to most areas of design is very competitive.

The following information is sourced from government statistics. The government's definition of types of job is slightly different to that used in this programme. For this type of job, the most relevant Government-defined occupation is 'Product, clothing and related designers'.

In 2001 there were 2,600 people working as 'Product, clothing and related designers' in Scotland. 12 in every 10,000 employees working in Scotland were employed as 'Product, clothing and related designers'.

***Entry Routes and Training:*** There are no prescribed entry routes into craft design. However, most take formal training courses from National Certificate up to Higher National Diploma or degree level.

Universities and colleges offer full-time courses in craft design. Courses may cover a range of craft subjects or main areas of study, such as ceramics, textiles or glass.

Those who find employment with manufacturers usually start in junior design or design assistant posts. Training will often be on-the-job with supervision from experienced staff. Initially they may spend most of their time doing drawing board work, gaining additional responsibilities as they become more experienced.

***Qualifications:*** Usual entry requirements for Art and Design courses are:

- some Standard Grades for National Certificate level

- a suitable National Certificate or 1/3 Highers for Higher National Certificate/Higher National Diploma level
- 3 Highers (A-C), normally including English and Art and Design, plus 2 Standard Grades (1-3), for degree level

However, entry requirements vary and alternative qualifications may be accepted—check prospectuses for details.

A central feature of the selection procedure for entry to any course in art and design is the submission of a comprehensive portfolio of work that demonstrates the candidate's potential.

Entry to all courses is very competitive.

***Adult Opportunities:*** Work experience gained as an assistant in a design studio or workshop, or in a design consultancy is valued. Commercial awareness and understanding of the rural crafts industry can be an advantage.

Suitable applicants aged 21 or over may do a college or university Access course. No formal qualifications are required to enter an Access course, but you should check individual course details. They lead to relevant degree/HND courses.

Many adults complete part-time adult education courses. Some of these courses cover areas where there are few full-time courses, for example embroidery and calligraphy.

Many colleges relax the normal academic entry requirements for adult applicants, especially those with experience in arts, crafts or design.

To enter this work or relevant courses, you need to have a portfolio of work showing your creative ability.

- 51% of people who work in occupations such as craft designer are self-employed.
- 20% work part-time.
- 7% have flexible hours.
- 0% of employees work on a temporary basis.

## Graphic Designer

Graphic designers create designs for advertisements, book covers, posters, magazines, company logos, packaging and so on. Visual design techniques can include illustration, computer graphics and photography.

***Work Activities:*** Graphic designers convey a message or create an effect by visual means, using illustration, typography and/or photography. They generally work on two-dimensional designs, creating ideas for book covers, CD covers, posters, stationery and captions for television. However, graphic design also incorporates three-dimensional work in the form of product packaging, exhibitions and displays.

Many graphic designers work for advertising agencies alongside copywriters, who produce the text. They design posters, newspaper, magazine and television advertisements and the layout for publicity materials and mailshots. Designers need to understand typography in order to give clear instructions as to the type and size of print to be used, as well as spacing necessary for illustrations.

Publishing companies employ designers to produce layouts, illustrate text and design covers of books and magazines. Designers are also employed to work on the general design of the publications. An illustrator prepares rough sketches and layouts, experimenting with different ideas. Dummy pages are produced and discussed with the client, printer and typesetter.

Designers who work in television, video and films, may have previous experience of book illustration or computer graphics. They produce credit sequences at the beginning and end of a programme and create logos, cartoons and illustrations for sports and news items. Sometimes their work extends to the design of props such as foreign currency, charts and special effects.

Computer graphics is an aspect of graphic design that has expanded rapidly in recent years. Designers who have trained in graphics learn how to become proficient in using computers to create visual images. Examples of computer graphics' applications include the production of audiovisual slides (a major area of work), improving the quality of animated film, desktop publishing, illustration and the look of websites.

Technical graphics requires accuracy and attention to detail, but offers less scope for creativity. Designers prepare plans and drawings from written specifications for use by scientists, engineers and architects.

***Personal Qualities and Skills:*** As a graphic designer, you will need to understand the use of shape, colour, space and form. Originality and imagination are especially important in non-technical work. You will have to be able to work under pressure and balance creativity against cost effectiveness. It is becoming more common for graphic designers to need a knowledge of design related computer software.

***Pay and Opportunities:*** Pay rates for designers vary with the industry and responsibilities. The pay rates given below are approximate. Graphic designers earn in the range of £15,000—£18,000 a year, rising to £22,000—£28,000. Higher earners can make around £36,000 a year.

Graphic designers work a basic 39-hour week, Monday to Friday. Working hours for self-employed designers may be irregular, depending on how much work they have week-to-week. Late finishes and work at weekends may be required from time to time, especially as deadlines approach.

Employers throughout the UK are:

- advertising agencies
- graphic design studios
- publishing companies
- traditional print and electronic publishing
- companies in the broadcast media.

Other opportunities exist in local government, in design departments of commercial companies and in design consultancies. For the experienced graphic designer, self-employment and freelance work are possible.

Entry to most areas of design is very competitive.

The following information is sourced from government statistics. The government's definition of types of job is slightly different to that used in this programme. For this type of job, the most relevant Government-defined occupation is 'Graphic designers'.

In 2001 there were 4,600 people working as 'Graphic designers' in Scotland. 21 in every 10,000 employees working in Scotland were employed as 'Graphic designers'.

***Entry Routes and Training:*** The majority of graphic designers have a degree or Higher National Diploma in an appropriate subject.

***Qualifications:*** Usual entry requirements for Art and Design courses are:

- some Standard Grades for National Certificate level
- a suitable National Certificate or 1/3 Highers for Higher National Certificate/Higher National Diploma level
- 3 Highers (A-C), normally including English and Art and Design and 2 Standard grades (1-3) including for degree level

However, entry requirements vary between courses and alternative qualifications may be accepted—check prospectuses for details.

A central feature of the selection procedure for admission to any course in Art and Design is the submission of a comprehensive portfolio of work which demonstrates the candidate's potential. Entry to all courses is very competitive.

***Adult Opportunities:*** Employers value work experience gained as an assistant in a design studio or in a design consultancy. Experience in related fields, such as advertising or marketing is also useful. Commercial awareness and an understanding of the industry you wish to work in is an advantage.

Suitable applicants aged 21 or over may do a college or university Access course. No formal qualifications are required to enter an Access course, but you should check individual course details. They lead to relevant degree/HND courses.

Many colleges relax the normal academic entry requirements for applicants with experience in arts, crafts or design.

To enter this work or relevant courses, you normally need a portfolio of work showing your creative ability.

- 37% of people in occupations such as graphic designer are self-employed.
- 10% work part-time.

- 10% have flexible hours.
- 3% of employees work on a temporary basis.

## Graphics Studio Assistant

Graphics studio assistants work for professional designers. They help to create a visual message using lettering, drawings and photographs. As there are few vacancies, entry can be competitive.

***Work Activities:*** A graphics studio assistant works under the direction of a more experienced designer, preparing clients' visuals and art work ready for reproduction into print.

The aim of graphic design is to communicate ideas by visual means. The graphics studio assistant visualises ideas through print, drawings, patterns and photography using a variety of materials, for example oil paints, pastels, crayons and acrylics.

Whilst the precise nature of the work varies from one design studio to another, each project usually involves similar stages. The graphics studio assistant takes instructions for the project and then researches the background. For example, they may need to look at a product to be advertised, the client company's image and the intended market.

They then work on creative ideas, producing rough sketches and preparing layouts. The graphics studio assistant may also be expected to present ideas to clients before preparing the work for production. Computer-aided design (CAD) is increasingly being used by graphics studio assistants. In undertaking a project the graphics studio assistant should always be aware of the cost limits and the suitability of different materials, techniques and reproduction methods. A knowledge of typography is essential in all aspects of graphic design.

***Personal Qualities and Skills:*** While you should have a good sense of colour and shape, the level of drawing ability and illustration required will depend upon the specialist field within the studio. Effective communication with colleagues and clients is important and you must be able to work quickly under pressure. You should also have a lively and enquiring mind and the ability to work neatly while paying close attention to detail. You will also need computer-aided design (CAD) operation skills.

***Pay and Opportunities:*** Pay rates for graphics studio assistants vary with the industry and responsibilities. Graphics studio assistants earn in the range of £11,500—£13,000 a year, rising to £14,500—£17,000. Higher earners can make around £22,000 a year.

Graphic studio assistants work a basic 39-hour week, Monday to Friday. However, late finishes and weekend work may be required, especially as deadlines approach.

Employers throughout the UK are small commercial design studios, advertising agencies, exhibition companies, firms involved with point of sale and display, television, film and audio visual companies and publicity departments in large organisations. Entry to this work is very competitive.

The following information is sourced from government statistics. The government's definition of types of job is slightly different to that used in this programme. For this type of job, the most relevant Government-defined occupation is 'Photographers and audiovisual equipment operators'.

In 2001 there were 3,000 people working as 'Photographers and audiovisual equipment operators' in Scotland. 14 in every 10,000 employees working in Scotland were employed as 'Photographers and audiovisual equipment operators'.

***Entry and Routes Training:*** Most people enter this work after a high level course such as a Higher National Diploma or degree.

***Qualifications:*** Usual entry qualifications for Art and Design courses are:

- some Standard Grades for National Certificate level
- a suitable National Certificate or 1/3 Highers for Higher National Certificate/Higher National Diploma level
- 3 Highers (A-C), normally including English and Art and Design, plus 2 Standard Grades (1-3), for degree level.

However, entry requirements vary between courses and alternative qualifications may be accepted—check prospectuses for details.

A central feature of the selection procedure for admission to any course in Art and Design is the submission of a comprehensive portfolio of work which demonstrates a candidate's potential. Entry to all courses is very competitive.

***Adult Opportunities:*** Experience in using desktop publishing (DTP) software can be an advantage.

Suitable applicants aged 21 or over may do a college or university Access course. No formal qualifications are required to enter an Access course, but you should check individual course details. They lead to relevant degree/HND courses.

Many colleges relax the normal academic entry requirements for applicants with experience in arts, crafts or design.

To enter this work or relevant courses you need to have a portfolio of work demonstrating your creative ability.

- 22% of people in occupations such as graphics assistant work part-time.
- 9% have flexible hours.
- 2% work on a temporary basis.

### *Designer*

Designers are responsible for making sure that the things we need in our everyday lives are useful and look good. Designers can work in areas such as textiles, fashion, graphic design, product design or interior design.

***Work Activities:*** Look around at the things we all take for granted. Televisions, furniture, clothes, food wrappers, magazines—these things have all been designed by someone. Designers are responsible for making sure that the things we use every day are not only useful but also look good.

There are a number of different design areas. These can be grouped in the following way:

- Fashion and textile design (clothing, jewellery, shoes, carpets)

- Graphic design (using illustration, print and photography to convey a message)
- Product design (furniture, domestic appliances, cars, ceramics)
- Interior design (homes, offices, exhibitions).

In each of these areas designers might work in industry, designing things for mass production, or on small scale projects in workshops, either on their own or with just a few other people (sometimes called designer-craftwork).

Designers working in all areas go through similar stages in their work. It is important that designers have an understanding of who they are designing for—what does the customer want? How will they use it? The first stage therefore is to do some research. They also think about other factors such as what other products are on the market, what would be the best materials to use, how much it will cost to make and how easy it will be to produce.

When they have all the information they need, the designers can go ahead and produce a series of drawings and rough sketches to show to the client. If these are accepted, they come up with a finished design and sometimes a working model or prototype. If the designer is working in industry these will be passed onto production staff who use them to make the finished product. Designers working on small scale projects often have to make the finished item themselves.

***Personal Qualities and Skills:*** As a designer, you will need to be artistic and have original ideas. Drawing skills are vital. You will also need an appreciation of colour, shape and form. In many areas of design it is important to have some technical knowledge, for example the properties of the different materials you might use.

Good communication skills are always helpful—designers need to work with clients and other professionals. Self-employed designers will need business skills so that they can do costing and pricing, sales and marketing and book-keeping.

***Pay and Opportunities:*** Pay rates for designers vary with the industry and responsibilities. The pay rates given below are approximate. Designers earn in the range of £15,000—£18,000 a year, rising to £24,000—£30,500. Higher earners can make around £40,000 a year.

Designers work a basic 39-hour week, Monday to Friday. Working hours for self-employed designers may be irregular, depending on how much work they have. However, late finishes and weekend work may be required from time to time, especially as deadlines approach.

Employers throughout the UK include:

- Manufacturers involved in large-scale production.
- Firms involved in engineering and construction.
- Design consultancies.

Some self-employed designers work from home, or from studios or workshops, which they might share with other designers. Entry to most areas of design is very competitive.

The following information is sourced from government statistics. The government's definition of types of job is slightly different to that used in this programme. For this type of job, the most relevant Government-defined occupation is 'Product, clothing and related designers'.

In 2001 there were 2,600 people working as 'Product, clothing and related designers' in Scotland. 12 in every 10,000 employees working in Scotland were employed as 'Product, clothing and related designers'.

***Entry Routes and Training:*** The usual route into design work is through a relevant degree or Higher National Diploma course.

Entry to any course in Art and Design is very competitive.

***Qualifications:*** Usual entry requirements for Art and Design courses are:

- some Standard Grades for National Certificate level
- a suitable National Certificate or 1/3 Highers for Higher National Certificate/Higher National Diploma level
- 3 Highers (A-C), normally including English and Art and Design, plus 2 Standard Grades (1-3), for degree level.

However, entry requirements vary between courses and alternative qualifications may be accepted—check prospectuses for details.

A central feature of the selection procedure for admission to any course in Art and Design is the submission of a comprehensive portfolio of work which demonstrates a candidate's potential. Entry to all courses is very competitive.

***Adult Opportunities:*** Work experience gained as an assistant in a design studio or workshop, or in a design consultancy is valued. Experience in related fields such as advertising or marketing is also useful. Commercial awareness and an understanding of the industry you wish to work in is an advantage.

Suitable applicants aged 21 or over may do a college or university Access course. No formal qualifications are required to enter an Access course, but you should check individual course details. They lead to relevant degree/HND courses.

Many colleges relax the normal academic requirements for applicants with experience in arts, crafts or design.

To enter this work or relevant courses, you need to have a portfolio of work demonstrating your creative ability.

- 51% of people in occupations such as designer are self-employed.
- 20% work part-time.
- 7% have flexible hours.

## Footwear Designer

*Also known as:* Designer, Footwear.

*Shoe Designer*

Footwear designers create new footwear designs or modify existing ones. As well as keeping up-to-date with fashion trends and the needs of buyers, a knowledge of the anatomy of the foot is important.

***Work Activities:*** Footwear designers design new shoe styles or change existing ones. The designer needs to follow changes in colour and dress fashion to ensure that the company they work for offers up-to-date styles to the client. They also need to know the anatomy of the foot.

The designer helps to specify heel height, colour, material and last (model of the shoe's shape). They modify the line (or style) by adding or altering markings, punching, lacing and other details. For each line the designer produces about half a dozen possible adaptations from which the production manager and buyers can select the most marketable. A design may be accepted immediately, in which case sample pairs are produced to show retail buyers. Equally, the designer's ideas may be rejected outright. Frequently, the design is accepted provided changes are made.

Experienced designers are given the freedom to develop new styles. Such opportunities are more likely to arise in firms producing fashion footwear rather than classic or purely practical footwear. All new designs have to be approved by the management and sales team.

For both adaptations and new styles the designer produces a pair or half-pair of shoes. Starting from a sketch, the designer makes a paper pattern using a last and masking tape. Alternatively, designers may design directly onto a computer-aided design (CAD) system. Experienced operatives make up the shoe and after each stage the designer discusses any difficulties with operatives and craftspeople. Usually the designer or trainee completes the sample by adding details such as markings.

Designers need to understand the materials, machines and processes involved in production in order to design footwear that is practical and economic to manufacture. Trade literature, publicity material produced by top designers, plus visits to national and international trade fairs enable designers to keep up-to-date with fashions.

***Personal Qualities and Skills:*** As an aspiring designer, you will need to be creative and good with your hands. The pattern making aspect of the work requires great care to ensure that measurements are precise. Communication skills are useful in persuading managers and buyers of the value of designs.

You must be prepared to accept criticism and deal with the frustration of having your work rejected or adapted.

***Pay and Opportunities:*** Pay rates for footwear designers vary with employer and responsibilities. The pay rates given below are approximate. Footwear designers earn in the range of £16,500—£21,000 a year, rising to £29,000—£37,000. Higher earners can make around £40,500 a year.

Employed footwear designers work a basic 39-hour week, Monday to Friday. Working hours for self-employed designers may be irregular, depending on the project they are working on. Late finishes and weekend work may be required from time to time, especially as deadlines approach.

Employers include footwear manufacturers, retailers, agents and design studios. Some designers work as self-employed, freelance footwear designers. Entry to this area of work is very competitive.

The following information is sourced from government statistics. The government's definition of types of job is slightly different to that used in this programme. For this type of job, the most relevant Government-defined occupation is 'Product, clothing and related designers'.

In 2001 there were 2,600 people working as 'Product, clothing and related designers' in Scotland. 12 in every 10,000 employees working in Scotland were employed as 'Product, clothing and related designers'.

***Entry Routes and Training:*** Footwear designers normally enter the job with a degree or HND in Art and Design or a related subject. Some Fashion Design degree courses feature options in footwear design.

Specialist degrees are available at:

- De Montfort University: Footwear Design
- University of Northampton: Fashion (Footwear & Accessories)
- University of Arts London: Fashion Design Technology (Footwear)

The University of the Arts London offers a postgraduate qualification in fashion footwear. For entry students need a good Honours degree in a related subject or an equivalent qualification or at least 3 years industrial experience at an appropriate level.

***Qualifications:*** Usual entry requirements for Art and Design courses are:

- some Standard Grades for National Certificate level
- a suitable National Certificate or 1/3 Highers for Higher National Certificate/Higher National Diploma level
- 3 Highers (A-C), normally including English and Art and Design, plus 2 Standard Grades (1-3), for degree level

However, entry requirements vary and alternative qualifications may be accepted—check prospectuses for details.

A central feature of the selection procedure for admission to any course in Art and Design is the submission of a comprehensive portfolio of work that demonstrates the candidate's potential. Entry to courses is very competitive.

***Adult Opportunities:*** Work experience gained as an assistant in a design studio or workshop, or in a design consultancy is valued. Commercial awareness and an understanding of the footwear industry is an advantage.

Suitable applicants aged 21 or over may do a college or university Access course. No formal qualifications are required to enter an Access course, but you should check individual course details. They lead to relevant degree/HND courses.

Many colleges relax the normal academic entry requirements for applicants with experience in arts, crafts or design. To enter this work or relevant courses, you need to have a portfolio of work showing your creative ability.

- 51% of people in occupations such as footwear designer are self-employed.
- 20% work part-time.
- 7% have flexible hours.

## Textile Designer

Textile designers create designs for printed, woven and knitted fabrics. As well as keeping up with current fashion trends, fashion designers need to appreciate the technical limitations of textiles and production processes.

***Work Activities:*** Textile designers create designs for woven, printed and knitted fabrics and soft furnishings. A designer's duties vary according to where they work.

Designers who work for a small company may spend most of their time reworking traditional designs. For example, a designer working for a small worsted company, may be required to modify the design of an existing woollen cloth, perhaps adding an extra stripe to a pinstriped design.

Large design companies usually employ a small team of designers who create original designs. However, these designs usually have to fit a particular house style or image. In some cases, companies buy designs from freelance designers and pass them to their own in-house designers to modify and adapt them.

Designers will probably spend most of their time at a drawing board in a design studio. Many large firms now use computer-aided design (CAD) systems instead of traditional design materials such as pens, pencils and paints. Designers may travel to various national and international shows and exhibitions during the course of their research. However, this will often depend upon financial resources.

When they have finished the design, they send it to a print laboratory where a sample can be made up and passed on to the design director to examine and comment on. Self-employed designer-craftworkers usually make their own samples.

The designer may also be responsible for preparing colourways or swatches. These are small pieces or sections of the finished article that they can show to a buying team and retailers. These give everyone involved in the design process a better idea of the appearance and texture of the final product.

***Personal Qualities and Skills:*** Although some designers are not directly involved in textile production, it is very important that you have technical knowledge of yarns and dyes, as well as manufacturing processes and constraints, as this will affect your designs. For example, some machines may not be able to reproduce a lot of colours, so you will be restricted to using just two or three colours.

***Pay and Opportunities:*** Pay rates for textile designers vary with employer and responsibilities. The pay rates given below are approximate. Textile designers earn in the range of £16,500—£21,000 a year, rising to £29,000—£37,000. Higher earners can make around £40,500 a year.

Textile designers work a basic 39-hour week, Monday to Friday. Working hours for self-employed designers may be irregular, depending on the project they are working on. Late finishes and weekend work may be required from time to time, especially as deadlines approach.

Employers include in-house design units of textile manufacturers and specialist studios that work for a number of manufacturers. Some designers work as self-employed, freelance textile designers. Some designers work as textile/ fashion buyers or salespeople. Entry to this area of work is very competitive.

The following information is sourced from government statistics. The government's definition of types of job is slightly different to that used in this programme. For this type of job, the most relevant Government-defined occupation is 'Product, clothing and related designers'.

In 2001 there were 2,600 people working as 'Product, clothing and related designers' in Scotland. 12 in every 10,000 employees working in Scotland were employed as 'Product, clothing and related designers'.

***Entry Routes and Training:*** The usual route into this career is through a degree or Higher National Diploma course in Textiles, Art and Design or Fashion Design with a specialism in Textiles. These courses cover all aspects of textile design such as embroidery, woven fabrics or printed surfaces.

***Qualifications:*** The usual entry qualifications are 2 Highers for a Higher National Diploma (HND) or 3 Highers, normally including English and Art and Design, for a degree.

However, entry requirements vary between courses and alternative qualifications may be accepted—check prospectuses for details. A central feature of the selection procedure for admission to any course in Art and Design is the submission of a comprehensive portfolio of work that demonstrates the candidate's potential. Entry to all courses is very competitive.

***Adult Opportunities:*** Work experience gained as an assistant in a design studio or workshop, or in a design consultancy is valued. Commercial awareness and an understanding of the textiles industry is an advantage. Suitable applicants aged 21 or over may do a college or university Access course. No formal qualifications are required to enter an Access course, but you should check individual course details. They lead to relevant degree/HND courses.

Relevant courses in textile design subjects, at various levels, are offered by a number of centres, by distance learning.

Many colleges relax the normal academic entry requirements for applicants with experience in arts, crafts or design. To enter this work or relevant courses, you will need to have a portfolio of work showing your creative ability.

- 51% of people in occupations such as textile designer are self-employed.
- 20% work part-time.
- 7% have flexible hours.

# Bibliography


Albarran, Alan B. and Gregory G. Pitts: *The Radio Broadcasting Industry*, Boston, Allyn and Bacon, 2001.

Albrecht, Ulrich: *A Short Research Guide on Arms and Armed Forces*, New York, Facts on File, 1980.

Alexander, James: *Internships in Communications, Ames*, Iowa State University Press, 1995.

Allman, Paul: *Careers in Video and Digital Video*, New York: Rosen, 2001.

Anders, Peter: *Envisioning Cyberspace*, New York, McGraw-Hill, 1999.

Arkin, William M.: *Research Guide to Current Military and Strategic Affairs*, Washington, Institute for Policy Studies, 1981.

Baehr, H. and Gary A.: *Turning In On: A Reader in Women and Media*, London, Arnold, 1996.

Ball, Victoria Kloss: *Opportunities in Interior Design and Decorating Careers*, Chicago, VGM Career Horizons, 2002.

Barnouw, Erik: *A Tower in Babel: the History of Broadcasting in the United States to 1933*, New York, Oxford University Press, 1966.

Baucom, Alfred H.: *Hospitality Design for the Graying Generation: Meeting the Needs of a Growing Market*, New York, Wiley, 1996.

Baxter, John: *Australian Cinema*, Sydney, Pacific Books, 1970.

Beaman, Jim: *Interviewing for Radio*, New York, Routledge, 2000.

Berkowitz, Ira: *Vault Career Guide to Advertising*, New York, Vault, 2004.

Bertrand, Ina and Diane Collins: *Government and Film in Australia*, Sydney, Currency Press, 1981.

Bliss, Edward and James L. Hoyt: *Writing News for Broadcast*, New York, Columbia University Press, 1994.

Boella, Michael John: *Principles of Hospitality Law*, London, Cassell, 1999.

Bone, Jan, & Ana Fernandez: *Opportunities in Film Careers*, New York, VGM Career Books, 2004.

Bowers, C. A.: *The Cultural Dimension of Educational Computing: Understanding the Non-neutrality of Technology*, New York, Teachers' College Press; 1988.

Boyd, Andrew: *Broadcast Journalism: Techniques of Radio and TV News*, Woburn, Focal Press, 2001.

Brown, Douglas Robert: *The Restaurant Managers Handbook: How to Set Up, Operate, and Manage a Financially Successful Restaurant*. Lauderhill, Atlantic Pub., 1991.

Brown, James and Quaal Ward: *Radio-Television-Cable Management*, New York, McGraw Hill, 1998.

Bryant, Jennings: *Television and the American Family*, Hillsdale, Lawrence Erlbaum, 1990.

Buckingham, David: *Young People and the Media*, New York, Manchester University Press, 1993.

Buckner, Robert W.: *Site Selection: New Advancements in Methods and Technology*, New York, Lebhar-Friedman Books, 1998.

Caldwell, J. T.: *Electronic Media and Technoculture*, New Brusnwick, Rutgers University Press, 2000.

Careers in Focus: *Photography*, New York, Ferguson, 2004.

Carmouche, Rita: *Behavioural Studies in Hospitality Management*, New York, Chapman & Hall, 1995.

Carroll, Victoria: *Writing News for Television*, Ames, Iowa State University Press, 1997.

Cassiday, Doris, and Bruce Cassiday: *Careers in the Beauty Industry*, New York, Franklin Watts, 1978.

Clark, Mona: *Interpersonal Skills for Hospitality Managers*, London, Chapman Hill, 1995.

Clark, Roy Peter: *A Journalist Teaches Young Writers*, Portsmouth, Heinemann, 1987.

Cockburn, C. and Ormrod, S.: *Gender and Technology in the Making*, London, Sage, 1993.

Cohler, David Keith: *Broadcast Newswriting*, Englewood Cliffs, Prentice Hall, 1990.

Cracknell, H. L.: *Escoffier: The Complete Guide to the Art of Modern Cookery*, New York, John Wiley, 1979.

Craig, James: *Graphic Design Career Guide*, New York, Watson-Guptill, 1992.

Crawford, Tad: *Starting Your Career As a Freelance Photographer*, New York, Allworth Press, 2003.

Crouse, Chuck: *Reporting for Radio*, Chicago, Bonus Books, 1998.

Davidson, M. J. and Cooper, C. L.: *Women and Information Technology*, New York, John Wiley & Sons, 1987.

Delaney, Chuck: *Photography Your Way*, New York, Allworth Press, 2005.

Dennis, Everette E. and Edward C. Pease: *Children and the Media*, New Brunswick, Transaction Publishers, 1996.

Diamond, S. Taylor's Way: *Women, Cultures and Technology*, New York: Routledge; 1997.

Donald, Ralph and Thomas Spann: *Fundamentals of Television Production*, Ames, Iowa State University Press, 2000.

Dornenburg, Andrew: *Culinary Artistry*, New York, John Wiley & Sons, 1996.

Douglas, George H.: *The Early Days of Radio Broadcasting*, Jefferson, NC: McFarland, 1987.

Easlea, B.: *Fathering the Unthinkable: Masculinity, Scientists and the Nuclear Arms Race*, London, Pluto Press, 1982.

Ellis, Elmo: *Opportunities in Broadcasting Careers*, Chicago, VGM Career Books, 2005.

Faulkner, W. and Arnold, E.: *Smothered by Invention: Technology in Women's Lives*, London, Pluto Press, 1985.

Fensch, Thomas: *Television News Anchors*, Jefferson, McFarland, 1993.

Field, Shelly: *Career Opportunities in Advertising and Public Relations*, New York, Ferguson, 2006.

Foster, Timothy R. V.: *How to Succeed As an Independent Consultant*, London: Kogan, Page, 2002.

Fox Keller, E.: *Reflections on Gender and Science*, New Haven, Yale University Press, 1985.

Gardner, Garth: *Careers in Computer Graphics and Animation*, Fairfax, GGC, 2001.

Gibbs, Jenny: *Interior Design*, New York, H. N. Abrams, 2005.

Go, Frank M.: *Human Resource Management in the Hospitality Industry*, New York, Wiley, 1996.

Goldfarb, Roz: *Careers by Design*, New York, Allworth Press, 2001.

Gordon, Sandra R.: *Great Jobs for Film Majors*, Chicago, VGM Career Books, 2004.

Graham, Duane: *The Remarkable Story of Otto Graham*, Wayne, Immortal Investments Publishing, 2004.

Green, E. and Adam, A. Virtual Gender: *Technology, Consumption, and Identity*, New York, Routledge, 2001.

Greenman, Robert: *The Adviser's Companion*, New York, Columbia Scholastic Press Association, 1991.

Griffiths, D.: *The Exclusion of Women from Technology*, London, Pluto Press, 1985.

Hall, Ken G.: *Australian Film: the Inside Story*, Sydney, Summit Books, 1980.

Hewitt, John: *Airwords: Writing for Broadcast News, Mountain View*, Oxford, Mayfield Pub. Company, 2002.

Higham, Robin: *A Guide to the Sources of United States Military History*, Hamden, Archon Books, 1975.

Hilliard, Robert L. and Michael C. Keith: *The Broadcast Century and Beyond*, Boston: Focal Press, 2001.

Hinkin, Timothy R.: *Cases in Hospitality Management: A Critical Incident Approach*, New York, Wiley, 1995.

Holloway, J. C. : *Towards a Core Curriculum for Tourism: A Discussion Paper*, London, The National Liaison Group for Higher Education in Tourism, 1995.

Horstede, G.: *Cultures and Organizations: Software of the Mind*, London, McGraw-Hill Book Company, 1991.

Hungerland, Buff: *Marketing Your Creative Portfolio*, Upper Saddle River, Prentice Hall, 2003

Jain, S. C.: *Women and Technology*, Jaipur, Rawat Publications, 1985.

Jefferson, Michael: *Breaking into Graphic Design*, New York, Allworth Press, 2005.

Jensen, Clayne R.: *Opportunities in Recreation and Leisure Careers*, Lincolnwood, VGM Career Horizons, 2000.

Jones, Sue Jenklyn: *Fashion Design*, New York, Watson-Guptill, 2002.

Kieffer, John: *The Photographer's Assistant*, New York, Allworth, 2001.

Kirkham, P.: *The Gendered Object*, Manchester, Manchester University Press, 1996.

Kissane, Sharon F.: *Career Success for People with Physical Disabilities*, Lincolnwood, VGM Career Horizons, 1997.

Kring, Robin: *Party Creations: Book of Theme Event Design*, Denver, Clear Creek Pub., 1993.

Kurzweil, R.: *The Age of Spiritual Machines*, New York, Viking, 1999.

Lavery, P.: *Tourism Marketing and Management Handbook*, New York, Prentice Hall, 1989.

Lewis, Robert C.: *Cases in Hospitality Marketing and Management*, New York, John Wiley, 1997.

MacCloskey, Monro: *How to Qualify for the Service Academies*, New York, Richards Rosen Press, 1964.

Maclay, Edgar Stanton: *A History of the United States Navy 1771-1893*, New York, Appleton Co., 1894.

Mauro, Lucia: *Careers for Fashion Plates and Other Trendsetters*, Chicago, VGM Career Horizons, 2003.

McGuire-Lytle, Erin: *Careers in Graphic Arts and Computer Graphics*, New York, Rosen, 1999.

Miller, Samuel D.: *An Aerospace Bibliography*, Washington. Office of Air Force History, 1978.

Mitchell, Leslie Scott: *Freelancing for Television and Radio*, London; Routledge, 2005.

Mogel, Leonard: *Creating Your Career in Communications and Entertainment*, Sewickley, GATF Press, 1998.

Noronha, Shonan F. R.: *Opportunities in Television and Video Careers*, Chicago: VGM Career Books, 2003.

Orlik, Peter B.: *Career Perspectives in Electronic Media*, Ames, Blackwell Pub., 2004.

Packard, Sidney: *The Fashion Business: Dynamics and Careers*, New York, Holt, Rinehart, and Winston, 1983.

Parks, Peggy J.: *The News Media*, San Diego, Lucent Books, 2002.

Paullin, C.O.: *The Navy of the American Revolution*, Cleveland, The Burrows Brothers Co., 1906.

Perna, Rita: *Fashion Forecasting*, New York, Fairchild Publications, 1987.

Rachlis, Eugene: *The Story of the U.S. Coast Guard*, New York, Random House, 1961.

Reis, Ronald A.: *Careers in Art and Graphic Design*, Hauppage, Barrons, 2001.

Rocha, Tony L.: *Careers in Magazine Publishing*, New York, Rosen, 2001.

Rubinstein, Donna: *The Modeling Life*, New York, Berkeley Publishing Group, 1998.

Satterthwaite, Frank: *The Career Portfolio Workbook*, New York, McGraw-Hill, 2003.

Seguin, James: *Media Career Guide*, Boston, St. Martin's, 2006.

Sones, Melissa: *Getting into Fashion: A Career Guide*, New York, Ballantine, 1984.

Vogt, Peter: *Career Opportunities in the Fashion Industry*, New York, Facts on File, 2002.

Wilson, Wayne: *Careers in Publishing and Communications*, Bear, Mitchell Lane, 2002.

Yager, Fred, & Jan Yager: *Career Opportunities in the Film Industry*, New York, Ferguson, 2003.

Zahler, Karen Gantz.: *Superchefs: Signature Recipes From America's New Royalty*, New York, John Wiley & Sons, 1996.

# Index

## U



## V



## W



❑❑❑